The Adventures of Tosey and Banta

Gavin Malcolm Khan - McIntyre

ISBN13 : 9780993156533

Dedication

Sam Khan – McIntyre
My beloved wife who inspired and supported me in writing this story.

Story One

Tosey and Banta in the Beginning

Presented here are the stories of the life Tosey and her family. Tosey was always getting into scrapes, luckily this cat had nine lives like every cat, each life being being full of fun and adventure.

Tosey and Banta are a dog and a cat who are best friends. There owners are a young married couple called the Gywns, with whom they go off on adventures often ending up in trouble. Tosey being a cat has nine lives, therefore always manages to escape from hair – raising experiences.

This cat wasn't really a cat, more a kitten. This little kitten had never met its father but had a loving mother who gave her milk and encouraged her to make its way into its new world. She would catch kitten by the scruff of her neck if she felt she was straying too far from the litter, until she got to know her surroundings better. This world was a large, rustic kitchen on farm and in that kitchen also lived two Collie dogs.

Every day kitten, who had no name as yet, explored and discovered more about its first home. There was the warmth from the aga the round kitchen table and lots of cupboards to explore, a sink and plenty of noisy pots and pans. The farmer and his wife kept an eye on the litter and their children Rob and Jesse were always playing with and cuddling little kitten.

It had been a few months and kitten still hadn't left the house. One day the farm had some visitors. These were a young couple that seemed very much in love and seemed very interested in the litter, more than most visitors to the farm. The woman was called Sam and the man was called Kevin. Kitten liked them immediately, sensing they were sensitive and kind. They smelled nice too. She rubbed against their legs and curled up on their feet. Kevin looked at her and said: "What shall we call her?" Sam said with a laugh: "How about Puss in boots?" "Why not Garfield?" he said. Sam looked at kitten's white paws: "Why not call her Tosey?" "Tosey Wosey?" "All right, just Tosey for short then".

Sam and Kevin stopped cuddling kitten and moved to the table with the farmer's wife. It seemed to kitten that they were all getting on well, then there was some exchange of money and a handshake. Tosey was excited, something was going on and it involved her and this young couple. Kevin said to Sam: "would you get the carrier from the car?" Soon Tosey was inside it. She was a clever kitten and knew she was leaving the farm and going to another home with her new owners. She looked around the kitchen, at the two dogs,

her mother and knew she would miss them, although she was more excited about the adventure ahead and miawed in anticipation.

Kevin and Sam also lived in the country, although not on a farm but in a comfortable cottage on a large estate. Kevin's family had owned the estate for hundreds of years and as an inheritance as a younger brother had chosen the modest three-bedroom cottage overlooking a loch, located about two miles from the big house. Kevin's and Sam's cottage was ideal, comfortable and rustic with open log burning fires with a mix of today's technology and a by - gone era. Tosey had to start again without the help of her mother,

Although house trained by now, things were different, she slept on the bed some nights and some nights in the kitchen.

There were less farm yard noises but every few days there was a terrifying banging, this was the pheasant shoot but Tosey didn't know this. She soon got used to it however, and even began going to see the drama

5

that is a pheasant shoot. Kevin had planned to put a cat flap in the back door so that the now fully grown Tosey could stop being a house cat and enjoy all the adventures of living on a working country estate.

Kevin's brother Collin who owned and ran Castle Bloat was a lot older than Kevin due to a second marriage of their parents. Collin was a very capable man although a bit cold hearted. He lived the high life and was happy as long as no one deprived him of his luxuries. Collin didn't like cats and Sam was worried Collin might shoot Tosey.

Kevin had a job which it required him to get up early and drive to the nearest big town where he had a studio where he designed boats. Sam was a writer but kept her own hours. It was Sam that encouraged Tosey to make her first small step for cat but a giant leap for cat-kind by going through the cat flap. It was

still winter and there was frost on the ground. Tosey found the crisp cold air invigorating. Her nose
twitched as nature's scents surrounded her. Where would she go? What would she do? There was the
lawn leading down to the loch. The loch was frozen and something told her it was unsafe. Then there were her claws that so far had been driving Kevin and Sam buy scratching the furniture and their coverings.
"What were they for? There was a small bare sycamore tree in the garden. Tosey scratched the small trunk with her paws; she knew if she got up high she could see her surroundings better. So she jumped up at the tree with all four claws and found with more jumping and clawing she reached the first branch. This was marvellous. She now had a much better view of her surroundings and this basic instinct to climb would one day save one of her nine lives.

Tosey looked down from the branch and it wasn't till then that she felt scared. It was all right going up but looked a long way down. She called out in distress "meow meow" when suddenly seeing Sam come down the lawn. She had been watching Tosey from the sitting room window to see what the cat did. Luckily the cat was soon on terra firma.

As the months passed, winter turning to spring, Tosey got used to family life along with all the routines and

excitement of this loving environment. She looked forwards to Kevin getting home; when she would be getting her dinner, later lie on Kevin's lap while Sam and Kevin watched TV and discussed there day over a glass of red wine.

Summer soon arrived and the weather became warm. Tosey spent a lot more time outdoors, Sam and Kevin left the cat flap open so cat could explore the night and a whole new world. With her excellent eye-sight in the dark this helped her catch mice and rats and every night she would expand her world, and sometimes return with a field mouse to play with or a dead bird as a present for her keepers.

Late one night Tosey was exploring again when she came across a farm and round the back of which was a steading. She crept into this steading and nearly had a heart attack as she had alerted three spaniel dogs which began their barking. Luckily they were inside a kennel. This farm was where the keeper lived; not being a cat lover, so cat knew to avoid this farm in the future.

It wasn't in Tosey's nature to go down rabbit warrens or badger sets and she didn't know the different animals that lived in them. For example a rabbit holds no risk to encounter, a fox hole could be the cat's last breath, but a badger confronted by a cat may easily kill it. It was this third hole which Tosey didn't dare go down specifically but it was its investigating that nearly took her nine lives in one go.

A big female badger protecting her cubs had caught Tosey by surprise; this badger growled and bore a mouth full of sharp teeth. Tosey knew then that she would have to fight, so went for the badger's eyes with her claws and tried to look big. The badger lunged at Tosey and got a grip round her neck, the two animals rolled around but then Tosey couldn't breathe. She didn't have much fight left in her when suddenly the badger cried out and released his grip on Tosey. The badger scuttled back into its hole and as Tosey gasped

for breath she saw her rescuer. It was a Golden retriever and the dog licked the injured cat. The incident was to form a special relationship between the two animals.

This relationship unbeknown at the time would
take them on adventures lived by few pets.

Tosey had fully recovered from her incident with the badger and with her new found
guardian, the retriever, she could go everywhere with her head held high. This status
on the estate was probably what got her into her next escapade.

Story Two

Tosey Gets Catnapped.

The little cat was by the gate house to the castle, playing with the butterflies in the
rose garden when a red Transit van with bull bars pulled up just off the main road.
The back door to the van was open and nosey Tosey took a look inside. Suddenly
something big and soft came flying over her, covering her, it all went dark, and then
she was manhandled into the back of the vehicle. Tyres squeaked in the getaway, and
Tosey

called out in distress. The journey went on for a while, with some voices muttering in
an unsettled tone.

Abruptly the van stopped with a jolt. Its back doors were flung open. Still in her
restraints which turned out to be an old rug, she was man handled again. There were
the voices she recognised, plus one unknown voice. They were discussing a score and
someone said " you won't be disappointed, this is as pure as you get".

Tosey was trembling, the blanket was lifted off her and she found herself in a tip of a
flat. It stank, were rubbish bags were strewn everywhere, and unwashed dishes and
cutlery in the kitchen. The wall paper was coming off the walls, and there was dry rot
and damp. She didn't know but this was a squat inhabited by a drug dealer and his
girlfriend, being a squat people seemed to come in do something with tinfoil and a
lighter, then leave. The cat was miserable, she meowed and meowed, the man said
"shut up you; Lynda's not going to want this squeaking".

Called Lynda and Calvin and Calvin, the couple in exchange for drugs had got Lynda a
cat as supposedly a romantic gesture. Lynda turned up and had a fit: "what am I going
to do with that?" Calvin said "play with it

and stuff". Lynda looked at Tosey and said: "it's quite cute; I suppose it could earn its keep and get rid of the rats and mice".

This tone might have seemed alright to some, but after living at Castle Bloat with Kevin and Sam it was hurt her ears. Over the next few days Kevin and Sam got more and more worried about what may have happened to their cat. They presumed the worst; either Tosey was dead or had been kidnapped. First port of call was to call the pets rescue; they then stuck up posters with her picture on them, offering a reward of £200. Apart from searching in the road side ditches and hedges there wasn't much else the couple could do.

There was a third party that was concerned about the well being of Tosey and that was Banta the dog. He knew that his friend the cat was not on the estate. Without the aid of human devices it was his sense of smell and direction that finally led him off the estate and to a grotty town about seven miles from Castle Bloat. After hearing cat meowing in distress with the badger, he soon found the flat where again he could hear the distressed cat. Banta barked at the window and she peered out - at seeing her friend she felt relieved - knowing that with his help she would escape.

To the dog the only way out was to jump out through the first story window, about three metres high. After a lot of encouragement Tosey dropped down, then lay stunned on the pavement. Banta was worried he licked Tosey and suddenly the cat came back to life, jumping up, Banta was happy to be reunited to his friend.

For Kevin and Sam it was a relief that after four days, missing Tosey had returned. There was no obvious reason to them as to what had happened to Tosey. Of course it was something to do with the Golden Retriever who showed up with the cat. The dog had a telephone number round his neck, after calling the number Sam got through to a man who said: "yes it was my dog". It turned out he was the vicar and Sam offered him a reward, the vicar replied firmly "no" but said that it would be a great help if the couple adopted Banta

10

Kevin and Sam were surprised and asked the vicar what what had occurred which meant he had to give up Banta who was obviously a great companion. The vicar told the young couple how he was heading off to the Philippines as a missionary; he described it as his calling. Sam and Kevin were glad to take the dog and everyone was happy, especially Tosey, as they trotted around together everywhere.

11

Story Three

The Gwyns, a Dog, Cat and a Barge

Mid - summer arrived, and the Gywns - the family name for Sam and Kevin - had been enjoying a crisis free period since Tosey's was kidnap and had return. One day Kevin came home from work with a surprise for his wife, in the form of some holiday brochures. These were advertising canal holidays in the north of Scotland. Sam was delighted and looked at them straightaway. She needed a break from writing and also thought it might give her inspiration for her next book.

Tosey and Banta if they understood might have been worried that they would be put in the cattery and kennels, Sam voiced these concerns: " I suppose we'll have to leave the pets" but Kevin told her it was not like sailing which the couple had done a lot of -

this was a pet friendly holiday. Sam knelt down and excitedly patted Tosey and Banta: "We're going on a holiday and you're coming too". The dog and cat didn't understand Sam but by the way she was acting they both got thoroughly excited, with Banta wagging

his tail as hard as he could.

The holiday approached and Tosey and Banta both knew when their owners would be going away, having been left behind on previous occasions. There were bags in the hall, so it wasn't till Kevin said: "Come on

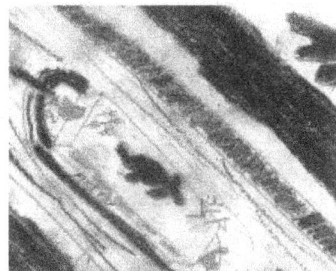

guys", picked up Banta's leash of its peg, and picked Tosey up and dropped her in the back of the car that the pets sensed this was the start of another adventure.

Kevin had an old school friend called Harry who lived halfway on the journey to where the barge was moored. They drove up the drive, lined with enormous Douglas Firs to a beautiful old mansion. Next to the drive way was a large stable block by the house. Called Evergreen Park, the house was similar in size to Castle Bloat, and Banta barked excitedly realising this was somewhere like home. There were a couple of Labradors hanging around outside, they looked docile and friendly, but once the family got out of the car the Labradors set of the alarm by barking.

Alice the school friend's wife came to the door, calling of her dogs with a 'down dog". Tosey had leapt back in the car but Banta wasted no time in making friends. Tosey was used to the keeper's scary dogs at Castle Bloat therefore knew that not all dogs were as friendly as Banta, but she didn't want to miss out on
anything, so she summoned up courage and got out of the car. Now that Alice was holding the dogs, Tosey had a chance to make friends.

Harry was playing Polo but would be back later, Alice suggested Sam, Kevin and the animals go for a work and she would prepare supper. As this was private land all the way down to the river a mile or so away, the Gywns could let the pets run wild. Banta was in his element sniffing here and there and fetching a large stick that Kevin threw him while Tosey looked optimistically at the huge Douglas Firs as if to climb

them, walked around them and finally decided she had found the ideal scratching post.

They walked for about half an hour down to the river where Banta went for a swim. Tosey was impressed but she also wanted to impress owners Kevin and Sam. There were no trees down by the river and she hadn't managed to climb the Douglas Firs, but there did happen to be a hole in the ground and it didn't have any bad smells, like the one at home so she headed in. For the first few meters down, with her excellent vision she could see where she was going, there were twists and turns and tunnels leading off from the main one. Tosey didn't think it was enough to just pop in and out of the hole, she needed to explore, so she continued further and further, feeling her way with her paws.

Suddenly the hole started to go up again and she was faced with a dilemma, whether to keep on going and maybe get lost in the underground maze, or turn back. She decided to carry on hoping she would come out a different exit to the one she came in on. It wasn't long before with relief, she saw day light and the sound of her owners calling her name. Coming out into the open she spotted Sam, Kevin and Banta peering down the other hole. Tosey meowed loudly feeling proud of herself, she had achieved her objective; everyone was impressed especially Banta who knew about the previous badger incident.

Soon it was time to head back to the house for supper and with everyone happy they made tracks. When they got back from their walk Harry was there to greet the family, he was in a good mood as he had won at polo. Kevin and Harry seemed to get on well, thought the animals, as did they with their newfound friends the two Labradors. It was a time of celebration for both humans and pets. Soon the food was cooked and then eaten along with some red wine. The kitchen was enormous and fitted everyone in the same room with space to go. The joint of lamb that the humans had been eating was only half eaten and the rest was put on the kitchen surface out of the dogs' reach to be put in the fridge in the morning.

Alice, Harry, Kevin and Sam soon went to bed, after long chat and some music, leaving the pets to do likewise. Now Banta and Tosey might have been great companions but they could still be naughty and the lamb joint looked and smelt irresistible. Banta tried to reach it on his hind legs but it was no good, Harry and Alice knowing that their dogs would try the same thing, put it out of reach. However they didn't have a cat, especially one as clever as Tosey, so when Banta treed for the meat again she scrambled up his back and leapt up onto the counter. Tosey wasn't interested in eating the meat, she did it more to impress her canine friends, so shoved the platter of lamb onto the floor where the dogs tucked in a feeding frenzy.

The next morning the Gwynne got up late at 10am and went down for breakfast, Harry and Alice were already up having eaten breakfast and were reading the papers. Banta was feeling guilty and so far hadn't been pinned as the accomplice to the lamb even though there was evidence all over the floor. Kevin and Sam apologized on behalf of their animals even they didn't know what had gone on. No one could blame Tosey but Banta got a telling off from Kevin before being put in the back of the car so the family could hit the road.

Their destination was the Caledonian Canal where their barge was waiting. They arrived at the barge at about 2 pm and it was brightly painted red and green and went by the name of Gypsy Queen. Sam clapped her hands. Banta and Tosey stared at it inquisitively and weren't sure whether they were meant to get on, but Sam made it clear by lifting the cat on board, then Banta jumped on. The barge had been rented for 4 day - heading towards Loch Ness and back. So they set off having brought all the provisions already and yes, it was as relaxing as it sounds - beautiful Highland scenery mixed with the joy of being mobile.

Tosey and Banta were allowed to go anywhere on the boat, their sleeping quarters were down in the saloon, they ate their usual food: biscuits for Banta and chunky meat for Tosey. The family's first their first day and

night went by pleasantly, the weather was clement but on the second day the sky turned grey. On a barge you don't really have to worry about storms although this was disappointing for the holiday makers, forcing them to stay inside and when the storm did come. The family were moored up and sat out the storm but weren't unable to achieve their objective in how much distance they covered that day

.

On day two and the weather was sunny again, the boat was chugging along just fine until they reached to a loch which is where the canal goes higher above sea level. Tosey spotted a bin bag in the water and heard something inside it. She was sure it was something in trouble. She could not swim so she encouraged Banta to help her, he barked for a while but Kevin and Sam were too busy with getting the barge through the loch.

F i n a l y , h e jumped into the water and swam to the bag gripping it as softly as possible. What now? He thought, there were 15 foot walls all round him so he let go of the bag and barked and barked for his life.

15

Kevin stopped toiling with the mooring warps and went to see what was going on; he saw the dog and the bin bag. First thing was to get Banta out. Now Banta was a big dog but there was no choice, so with the help of Sam he grabbed Banta by the scruff of the neck and pulled the dog on board. Next thing was to see why the dog had risked his life for the sake of a rubbish bag. Sam got the boat hook and hauled the bag on board she opened the bag and found four kittens inside, "marvellous, clever dog" she said, once again working as a team Tosey and Banta became heroes.

The kittens were all fine, Kevin now decided this was a good time to head home back the way they had come along the canal. Much as the couple and the pets loved the kittens, Kevin and Sam thought it best to hand them over to an animal shelter where they would be given to a loving family. The cruel truth was that whoever had previously owned the kittens had virtually left them for dead by chucking them in the canal.

The nearest town or city where the Gwyns could find a sheltered home for the kittens was Inverness. So
Kevin thought it a good time to wind up the holiday and motor back to where they started, also where their
car was parked. On a more direct route it only took them a couple of days to get pack to the car and it
Weren't the humans that looked after the kittens. Banta and Tosey were serious parents and treated the kittens with as much love and attention as their real parents would have done. The kittens weren't allowed on deck but they huddled together in Tosey's bed while Tosey shared Banta's bed.

The family returned to the mooring and drove to Inverness. Much as Kevin and Sam loved the kittens they couldn't fit four more cats under one roof so they were handed in to the animal shelter. By this time Tosey felt like the kittens' mother; when they were taken away she felt depressed and it was Banta that helped her feel better by licking her and wining softly.

It had been an eventful holiday and after a long drive everyone was happy to get home. Tosey was affected a lot emotionally by the kittens and although she knew she would never see them again she thought about having her own litter one day.

Story Four

Tosey and Banta out Shooting

It had been six months since the Gwyn family had their barge holiday. Tosey was now three years old, and had matured every passing month. As expected Banta had made a great companion, the pair had different lives; Banta being given daily walks from Sam and let out to roam the estate most days whereas Tosey had her cat flap and did as she pleased, quite often surprising the walkers by appearing from behind a tree or by popping out of a hay barn. By no means had the year been boring; the pets had left their home lots of times over this period, whether it be to go to the shops or to go and stay with the in-laws or a family friend.

Kevin had given up pheasant shooting as a young man, not because he disapproved of it but more because he was useless and more often than not missed the bird. Although there had been a time when he had fallen in love with a stray turkey and it became his pet. One day Collin, Kevin's older brother came round for tea, he had seen Banta from time to time on the estate and suddenly seemed quite interested in the dog. "Have you ever worked this dog " he said in his gruff pompous voice "Do you mean taking him shooting as a gun dog? "Kevin replied ' ' h e looks like he might be quite handy.

" Has he been trained?" said Collin, Kevin told him that Banta could sit, heel and fetch but as far as he knew had never been trained to pick up pheasants. " I'll take him out with me tomorrow; my spaniels will show him the ropes".

In order to see whether Banta would respond to his orders the two men took Banta for a walk in the grounds. Collin ordered Banta to fetch, go to heel, sit and most importantly they took the dog past the pheasant pen to see if the he would kill the birds before they had been shot. Banta knew what he was allowed to kill; mainly rabbits, hares, stoats and weasels and what he should leave alone; the pheasants, deer, sheep. Collin had to decide whether to ask Kevin to take the dog along to the shoot as he would be a beater, or whether he would take on the dog as his own picker upper.

Even though the Banta responded well to Collin, Kevin thought it more fun if Banta worked with himself.

There was an air of excitement in the cottage that night, Tosey watched as Kevin got out his shooting clothes which included his plus fours, Barbour, gloves, wellies and scarf. Kevin also watched the news, that

night reporting a good breeze and cloudy sky for the following day. This was encouraging - being ideal shooting weather without too much suffering.

Banta was sleeping when Sam came down early the next morning; she was preparing breakfast for her husband as a treat, fort would be a long tiring day out shooting. Sam had been to a few of the shooting days on the estate but preferred to do her writing that morning, and join the shoot in the afternoon. Banta was salivating; the smells of delicious bacon and eggs wafted to his sensitive nose.

He was ravenous, which wasn't unusual for him but when Sam handed him his dog bowl Banta noticed to his delight there was a lot more food than normal, so he wolfed it down even before Kevin arrived in the kitchen and started on his breakfast. Tosey had not been in the kitchen during breakfast; she was outside in the garden and only went inside after hearing voices and wondering why the rest of the family was up so early. Sam got Tosey her tuna chunks, which was a nourishing cat food; being a lot less greedy than Banta, she carefully ate her meal.

Also it was Banta's day and Kevin and Banta worked to the castle where all the shooters were having a preshooting drink. There was a good atmosphere pompous people drinking, laughing and speaking loudly,

most excitingly for Banta there were lots of other dogs. Tosey didn't like to be left out and left the cottage via her flap and followed Banta and Kevin to the big house. Tosey was aware that some dogs could be dangerous to cats so after seeing the pantomime of the shooting party, she trotted off to see one of her other friends on the estate.

Collin had reared a few wild turkeys for shooting and astonishingly Tosey had become friends with one specific Turkey. They had saved each other from a fox by teaming up to scare it off earlier in the year and now Tosey was quite often seen in the company this Turkey.

Througout the first drive of the day Banta had been behaving well even, though being a little over excited. There was only one dog that Kevin had had to pull Banta away from to stop a fight. Banta had also fallen in love and it just so happened to be one of Collin's spaniels; he had a flood of feelings running through him and was showing off by tearing around sniffing and barking. Once the drive started Banta had

to behave, it was hard work but a lot of fun. Kevin shouted "har, har, har" and banged a stick against a tree. As far as Banta could work out - a line of dogs and humans scared lots of pheasants out of the wood with sticks beating the trees and ground, white flags and barking. and on to the waiting guns. Banta was a good beater's dog; he must have scared at least twenty birds up on the first drive alone.

While this was happening Tosey was elsewhere on the estate with her friend the turkey, Tosey had heard the noise of guns before but never as loud or close; she had gathered it was something to do with the crowd outside the castle. The turkey seemed very scared and not without reason, it had run the gauntlet over the firing guns two or three times, some of the other wild turkeys had lost their lives this way.

The day went on and so did the bangs of guns, Tosey and the turkey were scared but didn't behave like the pheasants running to and fro clucking and panicking. The cat knew that the dogs and beaters might come
in to their wood so Tosey went about trying to find a suitable place for the pair to hide. The cat found a spot just in time, inside the hollow in a rotten fallen down tree. Their only hope was that the dogs would have too much else going on with all the pheasants running about and that their scent would be overlooked in the process.

The guns went quiet again and Tosey thought the shooters might be finished as the light of day was going down, when suddenly the whistle blew and the shouting, banging and barking went off into the woods. Tosey and the turkey had no choice but to stick with their plan, and hope the shooting party as it went through the woods would m i s s them, t h e i r lives would be saved for another day. Unfortunately the pair were discovered by a dog and just when Tosey thought it was all over, she realized it was her best friend

Banta.

What luck - they were saved, but not yet - one of the game keepers' dogs; an aggressive and much larger dog than Banta, had found Tosey and the Turkey. Now Banta wasn't much of a fighting dog but when faced with running away and losing his friends or fighting, he would fight. In response he put on his aggressive stance and growled; he wasn't scared of the big dog. Once again, and unbeknown to the humans, Tosey the cat and Banta the retriever together were heroes.

It was an unusual site: a dog, a cat and a turkey casually walking down the drive way that connected the castle with the cottage. Kevin and Sam who had by now had joined them, was still with the guns, they were enjoying a Sloe Gin, and wondering where the animal was. They were not too concerned though, assuming the dog had gone home on his own which was sort of true.

When they got home for dinner, they were first met by Tosey who came through the cat flap. Tosey was excited, wanting to introduce her newfound friend to her owners, and so she meowed and purred, then went outside again. Sam went to see what the cat was acting so excitedly about and thought she was seeing things as there in front of her was Banta and surprisingly there was this turkey as cool as a cucumber standing by the door. This was too good to pass up so Sam went and got her camera and took a picture of the three animals standing at the front door. She couldn't even guess how this scenario had occurred. Sam didn't really know what to do with the turkey but let Banta into the house then went to fetch Kevin

"Did you see the Turkey he brought home" said Sam, Kevin thought Banta must have killed a turkey and brought it home with him. There was no turkey at the front door and Sam realized it must have wondered off. So she told Kevin about the Turkey coming back with the two pets, Kevin didn't believe her but Sam had it on camera.

Story Five

Tosey and Banta at the Game Fair

It was summer again and things were as always in the Gwyn household. The pets, Tosey the cat and Banta the dog spent the spring helping or more often than not hindering Sam's effort to redecorate the drawing room. Tosey had knocked over a pot of green paint then Banta had walked through it and then proceeded to leave white paw marks all round the house. Sam and Kevin were livid and shouted "naughty dog" at poor Banta. However luckily by May had forgotten all about the incident and were planning to give the Golden Retriever a great day out.

Coming up was a sporting fair at Scone Palace in Perthshire and one of the highlights of the weekend was the dog show where pedigree dogs like Banta showed off their glossy coats and healthy postures with the hope of winning a prize. A prize like this was worth a lot to a breeder but any owner and their dog should be delighted with recognition. The Gwyns knew that it was unlikely Banta would win a prize even though he was of good breeding, but they thought he would enjoy making friends with all the other dogs and as they would soon find out Banta was quite the exhibitionist.

On the Saturday the Gwyns were up early for the weekend, Banta and Tosey were in the kitchen while the humans prepared breakfast for themselves and the pets. Banta realized he was getting extra rations and this usually meant he was going to be doing something exciting - and he was right. He watched Kevin and Sam load their picnic, wellies, and tweed caps into the car. As he hated getting left behind, and loved riding in the car, even if the couple were going to the shops, so without encouragement Banta jumped into the boot and hoped he wouldn't be told to get out. Next Kevin's waxed jackets, then finally the dog's lead were put into the boot as well. He ended up causing a bit of confusion, as Sam went looking for the pets after they had loaded

the car, shouting "Banta. Banta" around the garden and house, but when she spotted his wagging tail under the jackets she was much relieved.

Tosey was less enthusiastic about car journeys and tended to get in the way while driving, so Sam put her in her travelling box and the family were ready for the off. There wasn't much purpose for a cat at a game fair so the couple thought that as it wasn't too hot they could keep her in the car while they took Banta to the

dog show - later they would regret this!

The journey to Perthshire and the game fair went quickly and uneventfully, Kevin who was driving was fast but confident and he pulled over a couple of times to let the animals out to relieve themselves. They arrived at about midday and Kevin and Sam went for a saunter around the fair without the pets, just to check it out. They weren't going to be long as they had a picnic made up for lunch and they were already getting peckish.

Saturday was probably the busiest day of the fair and there were lots of country folk, Kevin would occasionally bump into an old friend and did the usual polite conversation. Back in the car Banta was getting restless; there were all these people and dogs rushing around having a great time while he and his friend were stuck in the vehicle. Suddenly he heard the familiar voice of Kevin who had returned with Sam for their lunch. The couple spent 20 minutes eating their sandwiches and boiled eggs, with a glass of lemonade, when Sam
said "I'll see you at the show Kevin". She was going to the champagne tent where she had found some old friends; it was going to be up to Kevin to show off their dog.

Kevin opened the boot and put Banta on his lead. After apologising to Tosey that she wouldn't be taking part, he strolled of to the show with the dog. Tosey was upset and decided that if she wasn't going to have any fun she would let anyone in ear shot know. Unfortunately the RSPCA were at the event looking out for animals in distress and although Tosey wasn't really in any pain she certainly sounded upset. There were two of them in uniform and one of them had a screwdriver which he proceeded to wedge open the passenger door with. Tosey's instinct told her these weren't necessarily friends and as she was stuck in a box she couldn't run. The two uniformed people didn't sound bad but they weren't her owners.

Back at the dog show Banta was behaving appallingly - sniffing and barking at all the other dogs whilst they all behaved impeccably. The show started and there were 20 dogs entered into the competition. Banta was due up in the next half hour. Meanwhile Sam had left the champagne tent to check on Tosey, on arriving at the car she found a note from the RSPCA saying Tosey had been rescued, due to neglect from her owners,

They had left a contact number. Their cat, on the other hand was not going to be taken from her owners that easily, so when she was being taken out of her cage to be put into the rescue van she wriggled and squirmed her way out of the so-called rescuers' hands and ran off free. Not really knowing where to go but in the past when in an emergency she relied on Banta, so she set off to find her canine friend.

Sam rang the RSPCA and asked about Tosey in a concerned voice and they confessed they had lost the cat. 'Great' thought Sam; first they take her cat then they lose it. As for Tosey, she had to be incredibly brave as there were dogs everywhere and she knew where there were more dogs she was more likely to find Banta.

Banta in the meanwhile was straining on Kevin's lead and just when Kevin began to think that he would have to pull him out of the competition, Tosey turned up. Kevin wrongly assumed Sam had let her loose but was still surprised to see the cat, and even more surprisingly, once Tosey turned up Banta started to behave perfectly. So that was it - there was nothing in the rules saying a cat couldn't be an escort therefore out to the parade ring went the three of them. Just at that moment Sam turned up to tell Kevin the latest news. She stared wide eyed, amazed to see her husband and the pets acting perfectly as they trotted out in front of the crowd.

The competition involved getting the dog to walk to heel, make it sit, wait for the command then come to
its owner then finally to fetch and retrieve. It was quite a site; Tosey who had very little training did exactly as Banta and both of them did every command perfectly bar the cat actually retrieving and fetching. Sam shouted her support and Kevin was glad that Sam had seen the spectacle. Once back stage (so to speak) the family was back together and Sam and Kevin rejoiced and showed their love of the two animals letting them know they had done well and cuddling them. Kevin asked unaccusingly: "why did you let the cat out of his cage?" and Sam filled Kevin in on the saga with the RSPCA. She said "we better let them know that we've got cat back" but Kevin replied that it was their own fault and to let them stew in it for a while.

It was not long until the prize giving for the 'show dog competition', even though the Gwyns knew they had the best response from the crowd, the judges probably would not give Banta a ribbon and it was only out of

curiosity that the Gwyns did not leave early and miss the event. Third place was awarded; this went to a large beautifully groomed glossy longhaired black poodle. Kevin thought this was their best chance of getting a price gone; so when second place was awarded to a Springer Spaniel they felt disappointed, there was no way the judges would find the Gywns rather disobedient dog with his bizarre companion a serious contender for the top prize of the day. The judge then announced on the microphone "and for first place

we award the threesome of Kevin Gwyn with his Golden retriever Banta and their cat Tosey". Sam jumped with joy and was so proud of her husband and their two pets, as Kevin went up with them to collect their ribbon.

"What a day" she exclaimed as they strode back to the car and soaked up all the attention from the public who seemed nearly as chuffed as they were themselves. Once in the car the Gwyns relaxed and Tosey, Banta and Sam went to sleep as Kevin piloted them back to the Bothy at Castle Bloat. It was as if Banta and Tosey were paying Sam back for making a mess of her drawing room and trailing paint all round the house earlier that year by adding their first place ribbon to the mantle peace.

Story Six

Tosey and Banta on a Camping Holiday

Another year had gone by; the animals were maturing but still had young hearts. Tosey was now four and- a- half years old and Banta was 5, it was every one's favourite time of year - midsummer. It seemed to the animals that life on the estate was getting repetitive, not that they liked brushes with death but they were keen on finding other exciting things to do. Kevin and Sam must have been feeling the same way or they could read the animals minds. One day Kevin came home from work with a bunch of holiday brochures, he absentmindedly chucked them on the kitchen table and said to Sam "it's about time we had a

holiday". Sam was delighted; the idea was spontaneous but was well timed. There were brochures for the Canaries, Florida and even a cruise round the Mediterranean and at the bottom of the pile was a brochure advertising campervan holidays exploring the Highlands of Scotland.

Sam initially thought Florida would be good, they could then visit Disney world but then Kevin thought that would be more fun when they had children. Then Sam thought about the Canaries but they had actually first met in the Canaries and much as it would be romantic, other than sailing there wasn't a great deal to do there, so then it became a toss - up between a cruise or camping trip. The holidays both had their appeal but neither Kevin nor Sam could make up their minds so eventually it was the animals that tipped the

balance and persuaded the couple to choose. It was the fact that you could not take animals on a cruise ship but they would be ideal in a camper van, plus the animals had not been anywhere or done anything in ages and deserved a holiday as much as anyone.

It turned out to be easy to organise, Kevin booked the van a week in advance, and then he got some road maps and marked all the places he thought the family would like to visit. This consisted of going through Glasgow then up the costal root via loch Lomond and Tarbot, where they would spend their first night, then they would go through Glen Coe via Ben Nevis and onward to Loch Ness and Fort William. From Fort William, they would carry on north to the island of Sky where they planned to climb the Culombs. Continuing to the very north of mainland Scotland John O' Groats and then make their way back through Inverness, Saint Andrews, and Edinburgh then finally, home.

So, it was a mild Sunday morning that the family set of for the highlands in the north of Scotland. As usual when the humans were packing their luggage and leaving it in the hall ready for the off, Banta did not know whether he would be going as well. As it happened one of the main reasons the Gwyns were going in the camper van was so they could bring the pets. Kevin had picked up the van the night before and it was now time to load the luggage, animals and hit the road.

The first hour or so was tedious, boring motor ways and as they approached and drove through Glasgow the traffic got bad and progress was even slower than the cruising speed of the already slow van. However once through the city it wasn't long till they got a taste of the mountains as the land became rugged and soon they got to the bottom of Loch Lomond. There was a fair bit of traffic on the small road but they were making good progress; by early afternoon they arrived at the first campsite.

Once settled in at the campsite, the happy campers tied up Banta outside and because the cat was good at getting free from restraints, they kept her in the van. After that, Kevin and Sam walked to a nearby pub, which was quite famous by word of mouth, for a bite to eat and a tankard of ale.

Both Banta and Tosey were disappointed to see their owners head of in such high spirits only to leave them behind. Banta started to bark, he decided that if he was not going to have any fun then neither were his neighbours. On top of that, there were mouth-watering smells from the other campers' barbeques and Tosey and Banta would not get to eat until morning.

There was a young boy who had been let loose in the campsite by his parents, he was to make Banta's night. The boy came up to Banta patted his head and asked him: "what's wrong boy?" Banta suddenly remembered

his friend Tosey who was looking out the van window. He looked sorrowfully at Tosey then simultaneously strained on his lead. The boy named Henry, was naughty and mischievous, aged about ten, with curly black hair and a cheeky grin. Those who knew him better called him Horrid Henry, he unleashed Banta and found the van door open, releasing Tosey too.

This was great for the pets and they worked their way around the campsite getting lots of delicious scraps left over by the other campers. Henry, proud of his companions, took them to where his parents had their tents. His parents were not impressed and asked Henry where he had got them from? The boy lied and said they were strays and he had saved them! the parents shooed of the two animals. What would Tosey and Banta do now?
Theydecidedtofindtheirownerssoofftheytrotteddowntheroadinthedirectiontheyhad

last seen Kevin and Sam head.

It was not far to the pub, the naughty animals would then have to find a way in. They could not read the 'no pets' sign, of course, but when some inebriated clientele opened the pub door the animals seized the opportunity and ran inside at once. Their entry was so abrupt that a busy waitress carrying plates of hot food sent them flying, screamed as the dog and cat tumbled into the bar. The publican was furious, and shouted: "Who owns these animals?" To Sam and Kevin's horror, they saw who these were. "I'm terribly sorry" apologised Kevin, jumping up off his seat, "I don't know how this happened." The publican said they would have to pay for the spilled food and that they were barred from that pub.

Not liking to lose their temper with the pets, the Gwyns did not know the circumstances that brought the animals to the pub. Sam said to Kevin "How on earth did they get loose and how did they find us at the pub? I'm actually quite impressed". Therefore, to compromise the pets missed their bedtime snack, but Tosey and Banta had already had their fill so did not mind at all.

On the following day the travelling family set of north heading for Glen Coe and Ben Nevis, some of the best scenery in Scotland. This took most of the morning; soon they pulled up at a car park of the main road with the intentions of taking in the view and stretching their legs. Kevin and Sam did not know horrid Henry. If they had, they would have noticed the little boy with his parents stuffing his face with a sandwich at the same car park. Henry noticed his friends Banta and Tosey and as they were let out of the car to go to the loo. Henry

went about petting the animals. Sam and Kevin were tired and realised the animals got on well with this boy so they said he could take Tosey for a short work but Banta was to prone to run off so he had to stay in the car while the Gywns had a nap.

It had been half an hour or so when the Gwyns were woken up by an angry looking man with a moustache and a small and worried looking woman with a frown. Kevin opened his window and said "hello" the man said "have you seen my son"? Kevin told them that he had let a young boy go for a walk with his cat half

an hour ago and was surprised he was not back yet. Everyone was worried as there was a mist coming down over the mountain, and their worst fears were that the boy might have got lost while possibly trying to climb Ben Nevis. As it happened, the two couples had reached the right conclusion. Henry with his companion Tosey had decided to climb Ben Nevis and soon found themselves rather cold and surrounded in mist. Tosey had followed the boy faithfully after all Henry had let him free

the night before and he had got a good meal out of it, but Tosey was not happy now he didn't know the way home and was scared and let it show by meowing loudly.

Back at the car park, the two couples were running through the options; call in the emergency services or head up the mountain themselves. Kevin had done a lot of hill walking, orienteering and climbing in the past so came up with a plan. He decided it was worth trying to find Henry and Tosey himself before calling in mountain petrol as the two of them couldn't have got far and if he took Banta between them they had a good chance of finding Tosey and Hendry.

Kevin had seen the direction the boy had set of in before his nap and explained to Banta as best he could what they were doing, as you know Banta is a clever dog and knew he had to find Tosey and he soon picked up the scent. Kevin and Banta did not walk that fast as the mist was getting thicker and Banta had to keep sniffing about, Kevin thought now that the best thing to pin point the lost explorers would be to shout and shout. He did so nonstop, until finally but faintly he heard a young boy calling back, "help!" The young voice shouted and five minutes later Kevin with Banta found the small boy and the cat. Although it was still misty, all four of them were safe back with their families forty minutes or so later.

The boy's father was furious, and his mother in floods of tears but ultimately they were happy to have their son back safe. Kevin was relieved especially as he felt guilty that he had let the boy go off with Tosey. Sam said to Kevin "I love you but can we go home now I think we've had enough excitement for one holiday" Kevin agreed, maybe they had. He turned the campervan round heading south for home and ultimately a good rest.

Story Seven

Tosey in a Rally

One day an old rally friend of Kevin's called up and invited Kevin and his family to watch him rally. The pets were coming too as there was no one to look after them at home.

Once at the event, they had to be were locked in the car, perhaps irresponsibly of the couple, or because they had to get some fresh air, they had left a gap in the window of the car and it was open just wide enough for Tosey to crawl out of. Tosey strutted round the service area and saw this bright yellow car with flared wheel arches and a spoiler; called a 6R4 it was probably the fastest car there. Tosey hid in the yellow car.

The rally started and Tosey loved the feeling as she sped along and to see more Tosey came out of her hiding place. The driver nearly crashed with surprise but decided to finish the rally even with the cat. The spectators could not believe their eyes as what looked like a cat co - driving in the winning car. At the end of the rally the cat was keen to get back to his family.

The Gwyns had been looking for Tosey, after eventually finding her had not an inkling of where she might have been. Therefore, when Kevin read his rally magazine he was speechless to see a picture of a rally car with Tosey perched on the dashboard the accompanying headline read:

SCOTTISH RALLY CHAMPION WINS RALLY WITH HELP FROM...A CAT.

The fact that Kevin used to rally and that his cat seemed to like it equally as much as he got him thinking. He was doing well at work and he had more money coming in than going out, so he said to Sam: "well why not take up rallying again?"

The problem was that Kevin liked to do most things as a family but Sam wasn't to keen on fast cars, there was also Banter to take into consideration. The best idea was to let Sam and Banter spectator. They could also take photographs at the services or pitch in with the mechanics if need be. This would give Banter a good walk going to some of the obscure spectator points and watch their partners race past.

It took Kevin some organising, he had to get a car and a co - driver, he decided that a classic rally car and series was more to his liking the cars were nearly as fast and more fun to drive. His dream car was an e - type Jaguar but they weren't designed to rally. However Kevin was stubborn, he wanted that car in those rallies. Therefore, Kevin found a mechanic who would build the car and add accessories like felt on the dashboard for Tosey to hold on to.

Soon the car was built, now to find a co - driver. When Kevin was young and had taken rallying quite seriously, he had driven with a professional co - driver. Now Kevin was not going pro any longer, he thought that perhaps his older brother Collin who also loved motor sport would like to do it with him. So Kevin asked Collin, who was delighted. He said: " You must be was mad to be rallying a classic e - type

but I also think its genius". Kevin omitted to mention to Collin about the cat, as he was not sure if Collin would go for it, not liking cats for one.

The rally was to be held in Wales and the team set of from Scotland in a big van with Kevin, Sam, Collin, Banter and Tosey with the car on a trailer. On arrival heads turned in all directions, what a car and who brought their pets with them. During the journey Collin, being quite well versed on rallying, said to Kevin that "I've had seen the cat in the last rally via a magazine, though, I'm slightly uncertain I think it might be good fun".

Tosey was on a high ever since the car had appeared at the house, it was better than a nip of catnip. Jumping about, she could not really differentiate between all cars but she knew the type of car that makes a lot of noise and goes very fast just like the 6R4. Banta on the other hand spent the whole of the last rally locked
in the car and did not have much fun at all, so he just wined a bit during the journey and secretly hoped he would not have to go in a fast car.

Soon the Rally had begun, Sam and Banta drove to the second service area but the others raced off to do a satisfactory first stage. It was a couple of stages till the next service stop so Sam and Banta went to a good spectator point. Banta found the cars racing past quite annoying and tried to bite the wheels of the speeding cars. Sam made sure he was tied securely to a tree while she snapped away with her cameras for a rally magazine.

Banta suddenly broke out of his lead and as he ran off was hit by a speeding car. He just lay there and Sam ran onto the track while another spectator flagged down the next car. It must have been a higher power that brought the next car to turn up with a driver co - driver and cat. Sam in tears said to Kevin "quickly can
you get Banta to a vet, he's still breathing but is unconscious, looks like there is blood

coming from his mouth.

If it had not been for the urgency of the situation it might have been even more comical, but time was against the dog, and everyone was worried that if he did not get the proper attention soon he might not live. They had to stop the bleeding somehow. One thing on the Gwyns side was a very fast car to drive to the nearest town with a vet. The worry was the police but Kevin took the chance and floored it. Ten minutes later the dog was safe, the friendly vet in dark blue overalls had carefully examined him, and other than concussion the vet said: "There was a little light internal bleeding, with careful nursing he should be back on his feet in no time, so don't worry, and he should eat light meals for a while". Kevin and Sam were very

relieved, they had no need to panic. They decided that in any future incidents, they would do some research first.

Weeks later the Jaguar had been left in the garage and Kevin had decided not to have such a dangerous hobby any longer, so had the car set up for fun runs instead, which were still exciting but and safe. As for

the animals, they might have to stay at home in future or Banta anyway, unless he decided that he liked racing after all.

Story Eight

A Boat, a Voyage and a Shark

Kevin had come to a stand still at work, there were just too many boat builders doing the same as him. He had to take a different angle, what could he design that was exclusive, that no one else was doing. Kevin

was sitting at his desk in the cottage; B a n t a was curled up in the corner with Tosey. Kevin loved his pets and was just thinking about how he would like to sail round the world but he could never leave the animals for such a prolonged period of time, all of a sudden, Kevin had an epiphany: ' Why shouldn't I take the animals? By customizing the yacht for pets like Tosey and Banta'. It was also a great business idea, as a niche market he would customise yachts for pets.

Kevin did not have to design a boat from scratch, he was just going to customise his own boat. He began to do some research into how a dog or cat might react on a boat in the sea. This meant taking the pets out on the boat and keeping a close eye on the animals to see what could be added to the boat to make it pet friendly even on long journeys on the high sea.

Kevin had to get Sam's approval, after all the pets belonged to both of them and there was an element of risk considering the Gwyn's yacht would not be set up for pets till after a trial at sea where they pets could be monitored. It could be argued that Tosey and Banta were being used for experiments, but knowing how much they love adventure I don't think Kevin could be classed as cruel. And with this in mind Sam agreed to the venture.

Sam and Kevin did not like to waste time, so the boat trip or voyage was put in to

action straightaway. Kevin got out his charts and started plotting a course. A public holiday was coming up soon, as there was going to be a royal wedding and this seemed the perfect time to set sail. Kevin had plotted a course from the west of Scotland over to Ireland. The voyage should take a day there and a day back, as long as the wind was good they could sail most of the way. The Gywns' boat was very attractive and if Kevin had not been
in the trade could be considered a bit extravagant for a young couple. It was white and red with a tall mast teak decks and was about forty feet long.

Once again, Tosey and Banta were turning heads, as Sam got the pets out of the car and took them down to the pontoon where Kevin was busy preparing the boat and loading previsions. One of the marine officials

approached Sam as she was walking down the pontoon: "We don't allow pets on the pontoon" he said , Sam, knowing that Kevin carried quite a lot of weight in the mariner, explained who her husband was and that
they were taking the animals with them on the boat.

Tosey had excellent natural balance and although not as enthusiastic as Banta looked confident but then Kevin said it would be completely different once under sail. Kevin had designed harnesses for the pets in case the worst happened and one or both animals were washed overboard.

The Gywns set sail with the wind behind them and all seemed well. Tosey and Banta were initially kept down below in the cabin and Sam watched them while Kevin manned the helm. Surprisingly Tosey seemed to be loving it, jumping about inquisitively aboard the vessel, whereas Banta was not having much of a good time and just lay down under the bed, watching her.

Banta felt sick, the relentless rocking was not helping. In fact he retched a couple of times. Sam told him "I hope you get your sea legs soon, then you'll enjoy the trip". She could tell Banta was not well and decided that he might feel better up on deck; after all, he had to appear on deck some time. It was a good idea the fresh salt air and cooling breeze made Banta forget his nausea. Next it was Tosey's turn to come on deck, this had the total opposite effect to Banta, Tosey cowed in the cockpit for it was too cold and wet for her outside. Sam put Tosey down below again; after all, it was easier to look after one pet at a time especially on deck.

They were a few hours into the voyage and the boat was handling well under auto helm, Kevin said: "methinks a spot of fishing is a good idea". He got out the fishing rod and secured a lure before casting the line. It was not long before there was a tug on the line and Kevin reeled in a small halibut, there was not enough meat on the fish to make it worth keeping, so rather than just throwing it back in the water Kevin felt ambitious. Using a halibut as a lure there was a good chance of catching something bigger like a tuna.

So once again Kevin dropped the line in the water, it was quite a wait about 45 minutes before anything happened when suddenly there was a tug on the line, and what a tug , Kevin strained over the rod and

with all his strength started to reel it in. Banta was not sure what the excitement was but it was infectious, so he stuck his head out over the side of the boat and began barking loudly at the water. Kevin strained and strained but on only really made progress when Sam grabbed the rod as well.

Suddenly there was a fish or should I say shark at the end of the line, without thinking and being too stubborn not to get a reward for all their work the Gwyns heaved it on board. The shark was about 5 feet long, wade about 35 pounds, and thrashed about with its razor sharp teeth. Kevin who was tired, lost his balance and ended up lying flat on his back on the deck next to the shark and before anyone could do anything, the shark had sunk his teeth into Kevin's chest. Banta went mad at the site of the shark and seeing his owner at risk in turn bit into the eyes on the shark's head.

As the shark had released his grip on Kevin Sam had to act fast she grabbed the spinnaker pole and shoved the massive fish back into the water, to her surprise Banta then went over with the shark. Luckily the dog harness did its job well and Sam was able to pull Banta quickly back (not being sure how long he could be swimming for) aboard.

More importantly, Kevin was in a bad way; the shark had punctured Kevin's lung and he was struggling to breathe. Sam was in trouble, she could single handed sail the boat but was worried her husband might die if he did not get the right help. As she knew first aid she practiced mouth to mouth on him and managed to resuscitate him. He was soon sitting up, and getting stronger. She then attended her husband's wounds and kept him warm without moving him too much while the boat was hove to.

It had occurred to her make a mayday call and radio the RNLI helicopter, but this idea was discarded, deciding that this would not be necessary nor helpful, after seeing that Gavin was recovering fast and he soon got back to back to his usual self.

She managed to get the got the yacht home with no hitches, while Gavin rested on deck, and kept an eye on the pets while getting a nice tan in the process. It was not long till the Gwyns were back home safe and sound with some unbelievable stories tell to their children one day.

Story Nine

A Cat, a Dog and a Volcano

That winter; Kevin and Sam had found an exciting hobby. It all happened on Collins' estate, an old mine shaft which not many people had explored. Obviously, Kevin and his brothers had ventured a few hundred feet down the shaft but all ran out of bottle once the tunnel got too tight and signs of cave - ins were spotted. It was different though when Sam and Gavin went down the old mine with their pets. That is where they had gone wrong before not having the eyesight that Tosey had and with the sense of direction that Banta had.

The result was a successful mission down the mine but there was a bit of disappointment, as it did not seem go all that deep and there was no hidden treasure. or not that they knew of anyway. Despite this, the Gwyns had caught the bug and Kevin went onto a cave exploring website and looked at books to see how to progress with this adventure. The obvious step was to join a club, so they did. Then there was a tuition period followed by a genuine cave exploring experience. The club had never really considered pets to go down shafts, underground

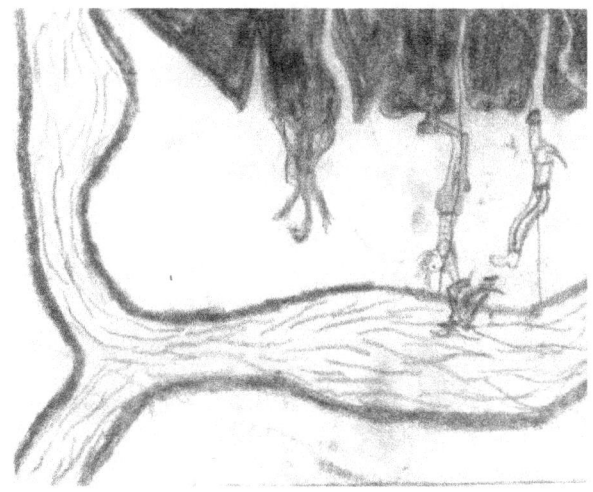

caves and rivers, but after Kevin explained these were not ordinary pets and he told his fellow cavers what the dog and cat team had done in the past - adventure wise. After this, it was up to Tosey and Banta to prove themselves, and prove themselves they did.

To proceed with an adventure at the same level as the last eight adventures the Gwyns jumped in to the deep end. Every explorer's dream is to descend down Mount Fiji in Japan and be lead into the centre of the earth, and the Gwyns, though relatively inexperienced knew this was their destiny. Some old folk law claimed the devil would rise from Mount Fuji and conquer the planet. This is not what the Gwyns thought but they did expect maybe to find some stalactites, underground rivers and breathtaking natural beauty, vast empty spaces. "Perhaps we might discover some ourselves in the process too" said Sam. "Um said Kevin, once we get good".

There was a lot of organising for the expedition: harnesses, torches, oxygen cylinders, dry suits, first aid kits. Tosey and Banta would be going, it would be easy to abseil the pets down the initial 1 stages but if there was any under water obstacles the pets would have to wait till their owners came back to pick them up. The Gwyns didn't really have a time schedule but they only took enough food and water for three days and nights underground.

Just climbing to the top of the volcano was challenging, but after leaving base camp early, the team got to the top at about mid -day. First Sam abseiled down deep into the heart of the volcano and once she got the first flat surface she tugged the rope and down came the pets, finally Kevin descended with all the equipment. It was very exciting; "what to do next?" said Sam. There were various options, to carry on abseiling down and risk running out of rope or to follow a tunnel that led off to the right.

The decision was made for them by a diagram and words saying this way. This was a surprise to the Gwyns as they thought they were the first explorers to venture down the inside of Mount Fuji. Any way the obvious thing to do was to follow the arrow pointing them along the passage. Once underground their senses felt different, there was no day or night just pitch black also there was very little noise. These basic senses were going to change again as the team descended down.

It must have been around day two when the first changes to the surroundings were seen. Banta noticed it first and the humans knew something was up because he was barking like a maniac. As they

proceeded, suddenly there was a noise, yes a trickling noise. Kevin said: "no it couldn't be, not this far down under ground".

Sure enough the team turned a corner and there in front of them in a big cavern n was a giant waterfall plunging into a pool. The torches showed up how amazingly pure the water was, not only was it crystal clear but also delicious to taste. This was a good opportunity to guzzle plenty water and refill their flasks.

"The water leaves the cavern down a steep stream m so why not take advantage of this? said Sam". " I have an excellent plan". It was decided that, having brought life jackets with them to inflate them, leaving the pets to find their way back to the surface, they all jumped in the water. It might mean not taking the animals and expecting them to find their own way home but Sam and Gavin knew what good sense of direction the animals had.

Plus there was a team of helpers camped out on the side of the mountain ready to rescue anyone that came within ear shot. With this in mind and not knowing how challenging the rapids would be, the pets were left on the bank and off went Kevin and Sam.

It was lucky they did leave the pets behind because, as the rapids became surprisingly violent and the pets would have surely drowned. Down and down they went and the deeper they got the hotter the water became. The couple had to get out as quickly as possible if they didn't want to get scalded by the increasingly hot water. To get out of the torrent wasn't that easy as there were no banks on the sides.

Suddenly their opportunity arrived as over a water fall they went and into a cool plunge pool, they dragged themselves out of the water onto a sandy beach and collected their thoughts.

Looking around, worriedly: had the person or people who graffitied the wall near the surface come this far, and if so did they die down here as they could not yet see a way to get back, or a light showing a way out

into the open. "However the graffiti does not show any signs of something like that, " said Sam, taking a closer look at it. "Perhaps it would show us the way out?" Kevin said. The strange thing was seeing more tunnels leading from the plunge pool cavern. There were piles of earth by the entrances to all two of the tunnels and there were claw marks in the soil. Could it be a sign of life this far underground.

There didn't seem to be another way out anyway so they would have to take one of the tunnels. Suddenly there was a big splash into the pool and to the Gwyns' horror and surprise out crawled Tosey, followed shortly by Banta. Well that was one thing the Gwyns should have predicted, after all the pets were amazing swimmers and secondly they hated being left out on any potential adventure. Kevin and Sam were delighted happy to see the pets, especially now there might be a possible predator down there with them.

The Gwyns decided it was time to find their way out, they had enough to report to the outside world and they would leave any further explorers with some good advice. Tosey worked out that his owners were lost and with his nose and Banta's sense of direction they were sure to find their way and return safely to the top of the world... The pets could also identify what the animal was that lived down there, it smelled like a mole, so it wasn't dangerous but at the same time it was enormous or a rodent like.

As they continued along the tunnel led by the dog and cat, Sam said "It seems we're going uphill". "yey" said Kevin. We made it". "and so did Tosey and Banta". Sam and Kevin drew some of their own graffiti with sticks and stones in case they planned a return trip, or for other cavers who may find themselves in a similar situation there.

It wasn't for 3 or 4 hours until he explorers got their first look at there underground horses, these were the size of a pony and seemed far more scared of the explorers than the other way around. The group stood there totally still for a few seconds then fled up the passage. Well that was it, they had found far more than they ever expected. Proof that someone or something had gone down the volcano before them; they had discovered an underwater river as well as a new species of animal. Sam took plenty of photos, with the

assistance of Gavin pointing out interesting aspects to photograph.

It was a matter of hours before they found there exit from the volcano; from where they were standing they could see the ledge that they had first abseiled down to. It was only 20 or 30 feet above them, and now as they were nearly at the top their radios could get through to base camp. Send down a rope the message said and soon enough they were all out of the volcano.

It was a matter of weeks later back at the cottage that the Gywns received a bizarre phone - call from an Australian claiming he had ventured down that same volcano 15 years earlier, but like the Gywns never reported the finds as he didn't want it spoilt by tourism. They were not sure whether they believed him, he sounded a bit young to have gone down there 15 years previously.

This is the last recorded memoirs of Sam, Kevin, Banta and Tosey, not to say it was their last adventure. After all they are all still young.

Dedication

Sam Khan – McIntyre
My beloved wife who inspired and supported me in writing this story.

Story One

Tosey and Banta in the Beginning

Presented here are the stories of the life Tosey and her family. Tosey was always getting into scrapes, luckily this cat had nine lives like every cat, each life being being full of fun and adventure.

Tosey and Banta are a dog and a cat who are best friends. There owners are a young married couple called the Gywns, with whom they go off on adventures often ending up in trouble. Tosey being a cat has nine lives, therefore always manages to escape from hair – raising experiences.

This cat wasn't really a cat, more a kitten. This little kitten had never met its father but had a loving mother who gave her milk and encouraged her to make its way into its new world. She would catch kitten by the scruff of her neck if she felt she was straying too far from the litter, until she got to know her surroundings better. This world was a large, rustic kitchen on farm and in that kitchen also lived two Collie dogs.

Every day kitten, who had no name as yet, explored and discovered more about its first home. There was the warmth from the aga the round kitchen table and lots of cupboards to explore, a sink and plenty of noisy pots and pans. The farmer and his wife kept an eye on the litter and their children Rob and Jesse were always playing with and cuddling little kitten.

It had been a few months and kitten still hadn't left the house. One day the farm had some visitors. These were a young couple that seemed very much in love and seemed very interested in the litter, more than most visitors to the farm. The woman was called Sam and the man was called Kevin. Kitten liked them immediately, sensing they were sensitive and kind. They smelled nice too. She rubbed against their legs and curled up on their feet. Kevin looked at her and said: "What shall we call her?" Sam said with a laugh: "How about Puss in boots?" "Why not Garfield?" he said. Sam looked at kitten's white paws: "Why not call her Tosey?" "Tosey Wosey?" "All right, just Tosey for short then".

Sam and Kevin stopped cuddling kitten and moved to the table with the farmer's wife. It seemed to kitten that they were all getting on well, then there was some exchange of money and a handshake. Tosey was excited, something was going on and it involved her and this young couple. Kevin said to Sam: "would you get the carrier from the car?" Soon Tosey was inside it. She was a clever kitten and knew she was leaving the farm and going to another home with her new owners. She looked around the kitchen, at the two dogs,

her mother and knew she would miss them, although she was more excited about the adventure ahead and miawed in anticipation.

Kevin and Sam also lived in the country, although not on a farm but in a comfortable cottage on a large estate. Kevin's family had owned the estate for hundreds of years and as an inheritance as a younger brother had chosen the modest three-bedroom cottage overlooking a loch, located about two miles from the big house. Kevin's and Sam's cottage was ideal, comfortable and rustic with open log burning fires with a mix of today's technology and a by - gone era. Tosey had to start again without the help of her mother,

Although house trained by now, things were different, she slept on the bed some nights and some nights in the kitchen.

There were less farm yard noises but every few days there was a terrifying banging, this was the pheasant shoot but Tosey didn't know this. She soon got used to it however, and even began going to see the drama

that is a pheasant shoot. Kevin had planned to put a cat flap in the back door so that the now fully grown Tosey could stop being a house cat and enjoy all the adventures of living on a working country estate.

Kevin's brother Collin who owned and ran Castle Bloat was a lot older than Kevin due to a second marriage of their parents. Collin was a very capable man although a bit cold hearted. He lived the high life and was happy as long as no one deprived him of his luxuries. Collin didn't like cats and Sam was worried Collin might shoot Tosey.

Kevin had a job which it required him to get up early and drive to the nearest big town where he had a studio where he designed boats. Sam was a writer but kept her own hours. It was Sam that encouraged Tosey to make her first small step for cat but a giant leap for cat-kind by going through the cat flap. It was

still winter and there was frost on the ground. Tosey found the crisp cold air invigorating. Her nose
twitched as nature's scents surrounded her. Where would she go? What would she do? There was the
lawn leading down to the loch. The loch was frozen and something told her it was unsafe. Then there were her claws that so far had been driving Kevin and Sam buy scratching the furniture and their coverings.
"What were they for? There was a small bare sycamore tree in the garden. Tosey scratched the small trunk with her paws; she knew if she got up high she could see her surroundings better. So she jumped up at the tree with all four claws and found with more jumping and clawing she reached the first branch. This was marvellous. She now had a much better view of her surroundings and this basic instinct to climb would one day save one of her nine lives.

Tosey looked down from the branch and it wasn't till then that she felt scared. It was all right going up but looked a long way down. She called out in distress "meow meow" when suddenly seeing Sam come down the lawn. She had been watching Tosey from the sitting room window to see what the cat did. Luckily the cat was soon on terra firma.

As the months passed, winter turning to spring, Tosey got used to family life along with all the routines and

excitement of this loving environment. She looked forwards to Kevin getting home; when she would be getting her dinner, later lie on Kevin's lap while Sam and Kevin watched TV and discussed there day over a glass of red wine.

Summer soon arrived and the weather became warm. Tosey spent a lot more time outdoors, Sam and Kevin left the cat flap open so cat could explore the night and a whole new world. With her excellent eye-sight in the dark this helped her catch mice and rats and every night she would expand her world, and sometimes return with a field mouse to play with or a dead bird as a present for her keepers.

Late one night Tosey was exploring again when she came across a farm and round the back of which was a steading. She crept into this steading and nearly had a heart attack as she had alerted three spaniel dogs which began their barking. Luckily they were inside a kennel. This farm was where the keeper lived; not being a cat lover, so cat knew to avoid this farm in the future.

It wasn't in Tosey's nature to go down rabbit warrens or badger sets and she didn't know the different animals that lived in them. For example a rabbit holds no risk to encounter, a fox hole could be the cat's last breath, but a badger confronted by a cat may easily kill it. It was this third hole which Tosey didn't dare go down specifically but it was its investigating that nearly took her nine lives in one go.

A big female badger protecting her cubs had caught Tosey by surprise; this badger growled and bore a mouth full of sharp teeth. Tosey knew then that she would have to fight, so went for the badger's eyes with her claws and tried to look big. The badger lunged at Tosey and got a grip round her neck, the two animals rolled around but then Tosey couldn't breathe. She didn't have much fight left in her when suddenly the badger cried out and released his grip on Tosey. The badger scuttled back into its hole and as Tosey gasped

for breath she saw her rescuer. It was a Golden retriever and the dog licked the injured cat. The incident was to form a special relationship between the two animals. This relationship unbeknown at the time would
take them on adventures lived by few pets.

Tosey had fully recovered from her incident with the badger and with her new found guardian, the retriever, she could go everywhere with her head held high. This status on the estate was probably what got her into her next escapade.

Story Two

Tosey Gets Catnapped.

The little cat was by the gate house to the castle, playing with the butterflies in the rose garden when a red Transit van with bull bars pulled up just off the main road. The back door to the van was open and nosey Tosey took a look inside. Suddenly something big and soft came flying over her, covering her, it all went dark, and then she was manhandled into the back of the vehicle. Tyres squeaked in the getaway, and Tosey

called out in distress. The journey went on for a while, with some voices muttering in an unsettled tone.

Abruptly the van stopped with a jolt. Its back doors were flung open. Still in her restraints which turned out to be an old rug, she was man handled again. There were the voices she recognised, plus one unknown voice. They were discussing a score and someone said " you won't be disappointed, this is as pure as you get".

Tosey was trembling, the blanket was lifted off her and she found herself in a tip of a flat. It stank, were rubbish bags were strewn everywhere, and unwashed dishes and cutlery in the kitchen. The wall paper was coming off the walls, and there was dry rot and damp. She didn't know but this was a squat inhabited by a drug dealer and his girlfriend, being a squat people seemed to come in do something with tinfoil and a lighter, then leave. The cat was miserable, she meowed and meowed, the man said "shut up you; Lynda's not going to want this squeaking".

Called Lynda and Calvin and Calvin, the couple in exchange for drugs had got Lynda a cat as supposedly a romantic gesture. Lynda turned up and had a fit: "what am I going to do with that?" Calvin said "play with it

and stuff". Lynda looked at Tosey and said: "it's quite cute; I suppose it could earn its keep and get rid of the rats and mice".

This tone might have seemed alright to some, but after living at Castle Bloat with Kevin and Sam it was hurt her ears. Over the next few days Kevin and Sam got more and more worried about what may have happened to their cat. They presumed the worst; either Tosey was dead or had been kidnapped. First port of call was to call the pets rescue; they then stuck up posters with her picture on them, offering a reward of £200. Apart from searching in the road side ditches and hedges there wasn't much else the couple could do.

There was a third party that was concerned about the well being of Tosey and that was Banta the dog. He knew that his friend the cat was not on the estate. Without the aid of human devices it was his sense of smell and direction that finally led him off the estate and to a grotty town about seven miles from Castle Bloat. After hearing cat meowing in distress with the badger, he soon found the flat where again he could hear the distressed cat. Banta barked at the window and she peered out - at seeing her friend she felt relieved - knowing that with his help she would escape.

To the dog the only way out was to jump out through the first story window, about three metres high. After a lot of encouragement Tosey dropped down, then lay stunned on the pavement. Banta was worried he licked Tosey and suddenly the cat came back to life, jumping up, Banta was happy to be reunited to his friend.

For Kevin and Sam it was a relief that after four days, missing Tosey had returned. There was no obvious reason to them as to what had happened to Tosey. Of course it was something to do with the Golden Retriever who showed up with the cat. The dog had a telephone number round his neck, after calling the number Sam got through to a man who said: "yes it was my dog". It turned out he was the vicar and Sam offered him a reward, the vicar replied firmly "no" but said that it would be a great help if the couple adopted Banta

Kevin and Sam were surprised and asked the vicar what what had occurred which meant he had to give up Banta who was obviously a great companion. The vicar told the young couple how he was heading off to the Philippines as a missionary; he described it as his calling. Sam and Kevin were glad to take the dog and everyone was happy, especially Tosey, as they trotted around together everywhere.

Story Three

The Gwyns, a Dog, Cat and a Barge

Mid - summer arrived, and the Gywns - the family name for Sam and Kevin - had been enjoying a crisis free period since Tosey's was kidnap and had return. One day Kevin came home from work with a surprise for his wife, in the form of some holiday brochures. These were advertising canal holidays in the north of Scotland. Sam was delighted and looked at them straightaway. She needed a break from writing and also thought it might give her inspiration for her next book.

Tosey and Banta if they understood might have been worried that they would be put in the cattery and kennels, Sam voiced these concerns: " I suppose we'll have to leave the pets" but Kevin told her it was not like sailing which the couple had done a lot of - this was a pet friendly holiday. Sam knelt down and excitedly patted Tosey and Banta: "We're going on a holiday and you're coming too". The dog and cat didn't understand Sam but by the way she was acting they both got thoroughly excited, with Banta

wagging

his tail as hard as he could.

The holiday approached and Tosey and Banta both knew when their owners would be going away, having been left behind on previous occasions. There were bags in the hall, so it wasn't till Kevin said: "Come on

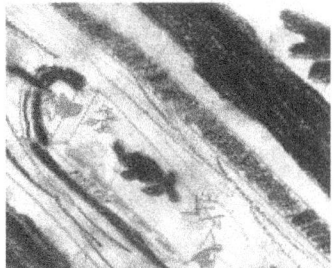

guys", picked up Banta's leash of its peg, and picked Tosey up and dropped her in the back of the car that the pets sensed this was the start of another adventure.

Kevin had an old school friend called Harry who lived halfway on the journey to where the barge was moored. They drove up the drive, lined with enormous Douglas Firs to a beautiful old mansion. Next to the drive way was a large stable block by the house. Called Evergreen Park, the house was similar in size to Castle Bloat, and Banta barked excitedly realising this was somewhere like home. There were a couple of Labradors hanging around outside, they looked docile and friendly, but once the family got out of the car the Labradors set of the alarm by barking.

Alice the school friend's wife came to the door, calling of her dogs with a 'down dog". Tosey had leapt back in the car but Banta wasted no time in making friends. Tosey was used to the keeper's scary dogs at Castle Bloat therefore knew that not all dogs were as friendly as Banta, but she didn't want to miss out on
anything, so she summoned up courage and got out of the car. Now that Alice was holding the dogs, Tosey had a chance to make friends.

Harry was playing Polo but would be back later, Alice suggested Sam, Kevin and the animals go for a work and she would prepare supper. As this was private land all the way down to the river a mile or so away, the Gywns could let the pets run wild. Banta was in his element sniffing here and there and fetching a large stick that Kevin threw him while Tosey looked optimistically at the huge Douglas Firs as if to climb

them, walked around them and finally decided she had found the ideal scratching post.

They walked for about half an hour down to the river where Banta went for a swim. Tosey was impressed but she also wanted to impress owners Kevin and Sam. There were no trees down by the river and she hadn't managed to climb the Douglas Firs, but there did happen to be a hole in the ground and it didn't have any bad smells, like the one at home so she headed in. For the first few meters down, with her

excellent vision she could see where she was going, there were twists and turns and tunnels leading off from the main one. Tosey didn't think it was enough to just pop in and out of the hole, she needed to explore, so she continued further and further, feeling her way with her paws.

Suddenly the hole started to go up again and she was faced with a dilemma, whether to keep on going and maybe get lost in the underground maze, or turn back. She decided to carry on hoping she would come out a different exit to the one she came in on. It wasn't long before with relief, she saw day light and the sound of her owners calling her name. Coming out into the open she spotted Sam, Kevin and Banta peering down the other hole. Tosey meowed loudly feeling proud of herself, she had achieved her objective; everyone was impressed especially Banta who knew about the previous badger incident.

Soon it was time to head back to the house for supper and with everyone happy they made tracks. When they got back from their walk Harry was there to greet the family, he was in a good mood as he had won at polo. Kevin and Harry seemed to get on well, thought the animals, as did they with their newfound friends the two Labradors. It was a time of celebration for both humans and pets. Soon the food was cooked and then eaten along with some red wine. The kitchen was enormous and fitted everyone in the same room with space to go. The joint of lamb that the humans had been eating was only half eaten and the rest was put on the kitchen surface out of the dogs' reach to be put in the fridge in the morning.

Alice, Harry, Kevin and Sam soon went to bed, after long chat and some music, leaving the pets to do likewise. Now Banta and Tosey might have been great companions but they could still be naughty and the lamb joint looked and smelt irresistible. Banta tried to reach it on his hind legs but it was no good, Harry and Alice knowing that their dogs would try the same thing, put it out of reach. However they didn't have a cat, especially one as clever as Tosey, so when Banta treed for the meat again she scrambled up his back and leapt up onto the counter. Tosey wasn't interested in eating the meat, she did it more to impress her canine friends, so shoved the platter of lamb onto the floor where the dogs tucked in a feeding frenzy.

14

The next morning the Gwynne got up late at 10am and went down for breakfast, Harry and Alice were already up having eaten breakfast and were reading the papers. Banta was feeling guilty and so far hadn't been pinned as the accomplice to the lamb even though there was evidence all over the floor. Kevin and Sam apologized on behalf of their animals even they didn't know what had gone on. No one could blame Tosey but Banta got a telling off from Kevin before being put in the back of the car so the family could hit the road.

Their destination was the Caledonian Canal where their barge was waiting. They arrived at the barge at about 2 pm and it was brightly painted red and green and went by the name of Gypsy Queen. Sam clapped her hands. Banta and Tosey stared at it inquisitively and weren't sure whether they were meant to get on, but Sam made it clear by lifting the cat on board, then Banta jumped on. The barge had been rented for 4 day - heading towards Loch Ness and back. So they set off having brought all the provisions already and yes, it was as relaxing as it sounds - beautiful Highland scenery mixed with the joy of being mobile.

Tosey and Banta were allowed to go anywhere on the boat, their sleeping quarters were down in the saloon, they ate their usual food: biscuits for Banta and chunky meat for Tosey. The family's first their first day and night went by pleasantly, the weather was clement but on the second day the sky turned grey. On a barge you don't really have to worry about storms although this was disappointing for the holiday makers, forcing them to stay inside and when the storm did come. The family were moored up and sat out the storm although weren't unable to achieve their objective in how much distance they covered that day, they snuggled up inside their boat and looked forward to tomorrow.

On day two and the weather was sunny again, the boat was chugging along just fine until they reached to a loch which is where the canal goes higher above sea level. Tosey spotted a bin bag in the water and heard something inside it. She was sure it was something in trouble. She could not swim so she encouraged Banta to help her, he barked for a while but Kevin and Sam were too busy with getting the barge through the loch.

Finally, he jumped into the water and swam to the bag gripping it as softly as possible. What now? He thought, there were 15 foot walls all round him so he let go of the bag and barked and barked for his life.

15

Kevin stopped toiling with the mooring warps and went to see what was going on; he saw the dog and the bin bag. First thing was to get Banta out. Now Banta was a big dog but there was no choice, so with the help of Sam he grabbed Banta by the scruff of the neck and pulled the dog on board. Next thing was to see why the dog had risked his life for the sake of a rubbish bag. Sam got the boat hook and hauled the bag on board she opened the bag and found four kittens inside, "marvellous, clever dog" she said, once again working as a team Tosey and Banta became heroes.

The kittens were all fine, Kevin now decided this was a good time to head home back the way they had come along the canal. Much as the couple and the pets loved the kittens, Kevin and Sam thought it best to hand them over to an animal shelter where they would be given to a loving family. The cruel truth was that whoever had previously owned the kittens had virtually left them for dead by chucking them in the canal.

The nearest town or city where the Gwyns could find a sheltered home for the kittens was Inverness. So
Kevin thought it a good time to wind up the holiday and motor back to where they started, also where their
car was parked. On a more direct route it only took them a couple of days to get pack to the car and it
Weren't the humans that looked after the kittens. Banta and Tosey were serious parents and treated the kittens with as much love and attention as their real parents would have done. The kittens weren't allowed on deck but they huddled together in Tosey's bed while Tosey shared Banta's bed.

The family returned to the mooring and drove to Inverness. Much as Kevin and Sam loved the kittens they couldn't fit four more cats under one roof so they were handed in to the animal shelter. By this time Tosey felt like the kittens' mother, when they were taken away she felt depressed and it was Banta that helped her feel better by licking her and wining softly.

It had been an eventful holiday and after a long drive everyone was happy to get home. Tosey was affected a lot emotionally by the kittens and although she knew she would never see them again she thought about having her own litter one day.

Story Four

Tosey and Banta out Shooting

It had been six months since the Gwyn family had their barge holiday. Tosey was now three years old, and had matured every passing month. As expected Banta had made a great companion, the pair had different lives; Banta being given daily walks from Sam and let out to roam the estate most days whereas Tosey had her cat flap and did as she pleased, quite often surprising the walkers by appearing from behind a tree or by popping out of a hay barn. By no means had the year been boring; the pets had left their home lots of times over this period, whether it be to go to the shops or to go and stay with the in-laws or a family friend.

Kevin had given up pheasant shooting as a young man, not because he disapproved of it but more because he was useless and more often than not missed the bird. Although there had been a time when he had fallen in love with a stray turkey and it became his pet. One day Collin, Kevin's older brother came round for tea, he had seen Banta from time to time on the estate and suddenly seemed quite interested in the dog. "Have you ever worked this dog " he said in his gruff pompous voice "Do you mean taking him shooting as a gun dog? "Kevin replied ' ' h e looks like he might be quite handy.

" Has he been trained?" said Collin, Kevin told him that Banta could sit, heel and fetch but as far as he knew had never been trained to pick up pheasants. " I'll take him out with me tomorrow; my spaniels will show him the ropes".

In order to see whether Banta would respond to his orders the two men took Banta for a walk in the grounds. Collin ordered Banta to fetch, go to heel, sit and most importantly they took the dog past the pheasant pen to see if the he would kill the birds before they had been shot. Banta knew what he was allowed to kill; mainly rabbits, hares, stoats and weasels and what he should leave alone; the pheasants, deer, sheep. Collin had to decide whether to ask Kevin to take the dog along to the shoot as he would be a beater, or whether he would take on the dog as his own picker upper. Even though the Banta responded well to Collin, Kevin thought it more fun if Banta worked with himself.

There was an air of excitement in the cottage that night, Tosey watched as Kevin got out his shooting clothes which included his plus fours, Barbour, gloves, wellies and scarf. Kevin also watched the news, that

night reporting a good breeze and cloudy sky for the following day. This was encouraging - being ideal shooting weather without too much suffering.

Banta was sleeping when Sam came down early the next morning; she was preparing breakfast for her husband as a treat, fort would be a long tiring day out shooting. Sam had been to a few of the shooting days on the estate but preferred to do her writing that morning, and join the shoot in the afternoon. Banta was salivating; the smells of delicious bacon and eggs wafted to his sensitive nose.

He was ravenous, which wasn't unusual for him but when Sam handed him his dog bowl Banta noticed to his delight there was a lot more food than normal, so he wolfed it down even before Kevin arrived in the kitchen and started on his breakfast. Tosey had not been in the kitchen during breakfast; she was outside in the garden and only went inside after hearing voices and wondering why the rest of the family was up so early. Sam got Tosey her tuna chunks, which was a nourishing cat food; being a lot less greedy than Banta, she carefully ate her meal.

Also it was Banta's day and Kevin and Banta worked to the castle where all the shooters were having a preshooting drink. There was a good atmosphere pompous people drinking, laughing and speaking loudly,

most excitingly for Banta there were lots of other dogs. Tosey didn't like to be left out and left the cottage via her flap and followed Banta and Kevin to the big house. Tosey was aware that some dogs could be dangerous to cats so after seeing the pantomime of the shooting party, she trotted off to see one of her other friends on the estate.

Collin had reared a few wild turkeys for shooting and astonishingly Tosey had become friends with one specific Turkey. They had saved each other from a fox by teaming up to scare it off earlier in the year and now Tosey was quite often seen in the company this Turkey.

Throgout the first drive of the day Banta had been behaving well even, though being a little over excited. There was only one dog that Kevin had had to pull Banta away from to stop a fight. Banta had also fallen in love and it just so happened to be one of Collin's spaniels; he had a flood of feelings running through him and was showing off by tearing around sniffing and barking. Once the drive started Banta had

to behave, it was hard work but a lot of fun. Kevin shouted "har, har, har" and banged a stick against a tree. As far as Banta could work out - a line of dogs and humans scared lots of pheasants out of the wood with sticks beating the trees and ground, white flags and barking. and on to the waiting guns. Banta was a good beater's dog; he must have scared at least twenty birds up on the first drive alone.

While this was happening Tosey was elsewhere on the estate with her friend the turkey, Tosey had heard the noise of guns before but never as loud or close; she had gathered it was something to do with the crowd outside the castle. The turkey seemed very scared and not without reason, it had run the gauntlet over the firing guns two or three times, some of the other wild turkeys had lost their lives this way.

The day went on and so did the bangs of guns, Tosey and the turkey were scared but

didn't behave like the pheasants running to and fro clucking and panicking. The cat knew that the dogs and beaters might come
in to their wood so Tosey went about trying to find a suitable place for the pair to hide. The cat found a spot just in time, inside the hollow in a rotten fallen down tree. Their only hope was that the dogs would have too much else going on with all the pheasants running about and that their scent would be overlooked in the process.

19

The guns went quiet again and Tosey thought the shooters might be finished as the light of day was going down, when suddenly the whistle blew and the shouting, banging and barking went off into the woods. Tosey and the turkey had no choice but to stick with their plan, and hope the shooting party as it went through the woods would m i s s them, t h e i r lives would be saved for another day. Unfortunately the pair were discovered by a dog and just when Tosey thought it was all over, she realized it was her best friend

Banta.

What luck - they were saved, but not yet - one of the game keepers' dogs; an aggressive and much larger dog than Banta, had found Tosey and the Turkey. Now Banta wasn't much of a fighting dog but when faced with running away and losing his friends or fighting, he would fight. In response he put on his aggressive stance and growled; he wasn't scared of the big dog. Once again, and unbeknown to the humans, Tosey the cat and Banta the retriever together were heroes.

It was an unusual site: a dog, a cat and a turkey casually walking down the drive way that connected the castle with the cottage. Kevin and Sam who had by now had joined them, was still with the guns, they were enjoying a Sloe Gin, and wondering where the animal was. They were not too concerned though, assuming the dog had gone home on his own which was sort of true.

When they got home for dinner, they were first met by Tosey who came through the cat flap. Tosey was excited, wanting to introduce her newfound friend to her owners, and so she meowed and purred, then went outside again. Sam went to see what the cat was acting so excitedly about and thought she was seeing things as there in front of her was Banta and surprisingly there was this turkey as cool as a cucumber standing by the door. This was too good to pass up so Sam went and got her camera and took a picture of the three animals standing at the front door. She couldn't even guess how this scenario had occurred. Sam didn't really know what to do with the turkey but let Banta into the house then went to fetch Kevin

"Did you see the Turkey he brought home" said Sam, Kevin thought Banta must have killed a turkey and brought it home with him. There was no turkey at the front door and Sam realized it must have wondered off. So she told Kevin about the Turkey coming back with the two pets, Kevin didn't believe her but Sam had it on camera.

20

Story Five

Tosey and Banta at the Game Fair

It was summer again and things were as always in the Gwyn household. The pets, Tosey the cat and Banta the dog spent the spring helping or more often than not hindering Sam's effort to redecorate the drawing room. Tosey had knocked over a pot of green paint then Banta had walked through it and then proceeded to leave white paw marks all round the house. Sam and Kevin were livid and shouted "naughty dog" at poor Banta. However luckily by May had forgotten all about the incident and were planning to give the Golden Retriever a great day out.

Coming up was a sporting fair at Scone Palace in Perthshire and one of the highlights of the weekend was the dog show where pedigree dogs like Banta showed off their glossy coats and healthy postures with the hope of winning a prize. A prize like this was worth a lot to a breeder but any owner and their dog should be delighted with recognition. The Gwyns knew that it was unlikely Banta would win a prize even though he was of good breeding, but they thought he would enjoy making friends with all the other dogs and as they would soon find out Banta was quite the exhibitionist.

On the Saturday the Gwyns were up early for the weekend, Banta and Tosey were in the kitchen while the humans prepared breakfast for themselves and the pets. Banta realized he was getting extra rations and this usually meant he was going to be doing something exciting - and he was right. He watched Kevin and Sam load their picnic, wellies, and tweed caps into the car. As he hated getting left behind, and loved riding in the car, even if the couple were going to the shops, so without encouragement Banta jumped into the boot and hoped he wouldn't be told to get out. Next Kevin's waxed jackets, then finally the dog's lead were put into the boot as well. He ended up causing a bit of confusion, as Sam went looking for the pets after they had loaded

the car, shouting "Banta, Banta" around the garden and house, but when she spotted his wagging tail under the jackets she was much relieved.

Tosey was less enthusiastic about car journeys and tended to get in the way while driving, so Sam put her in her travelling box and the family were ready for the off. There wasn't much purpose for a cat at a game fair so the couple thought that as it wasn't too hot they could keep her in the car while they took Banta to the

dog show - later they would regret this!

The journey to Perthshire and the game fair went quickly and uneventfully, Kevin who was driving was fast but confident and he pulled over a couple of times to let the animals out to relieve themselves. They arrived at about midday and Kevin and Sam went for a saunter around the fair without the pets, just to check it out. They weren't going to be long as they had a picnic made up for lunch and they were already getting peckish.

Saturday was probably the busiest day of the fair and there were lots of country folk, Kevin would occasionally bump into an old friend and did the usual polite conversation. Back in the car Banta was getting restless; there were all these people and dogs rushing around having a great time while he and his friend were stuck in the vehicle. Suddenly he heard the familiar voice of Kevin who had returned with Sam for their lunch. The couple spent 20 minutes eating their sandwiches and boiled eggs, with a glass of lemonade, when Sam
said "I'll see you at the show Kevin". She was going to the champagne tent where she had found some old friends; it was going to be up to Kevin to show off their dog.

Kevin opened the boot and put Banta on his lead. After apologising to Tosey that she wouldn't be taking part, he strolled of to the show with the dog. Tosey was upset and decided that if she wasn't going to have any fun she would let anyone in ear shot know. Unfortunately the RSPCA were at the event looking out for animals in distress and although Tosey wasn't really in any pain she certainly sounded upset. There were two of them in uniform and one of them had a screwdriver which he proceeded to wedge open the passenger door with. Tosey's instinct told her these weren't necessarily friends and as she was stuck in a box she couldn't run. The two uniformed people didn't sound bad but they weren't her owners.

22

Back at the dog show Banta was behaving appallingly - sniffing and barking at all the other dogs whilst they all behaved impeccably. The show started and there were 20 dogs entered into the competition. Banta was due up in the next half hour. Meanwhile Sam had left the champagne tent to check on Tosey, on arriving at the car she found a note from the RSPCA saying Tosey had been rescued, due to neglect from her owners,

They had left a contact number. Their cat, on the other hand was not going to be taken from her owners that easily, so when she was being taken out of her cage to be put into the rescue van she wriggled and squirmed her way out of the so-called rescuers' hands and ran off free. Not really knowing where to go but in the past when in an emergency she relied on Banta, so she set off to find her canine friend.

Sam rang the RSPCA and asked about Tosey in a concerned voice and they confessed they had lost the cat. 'Great' thought Sam; first they take her cat then they lose it. As for Tosey, she had to be incredibly brave as there were dogs everywhere and she knew where there were more dogs she was more likely to find Banta.

Banta in the meanwhile was straining on Kevin's lead and just when Kevin began to think that he would have to pull him out of the competition, Tosey turned up. Kevin wrongly assumed Sam had let her loose but was still surprised to see the cat, and even more surprisingly, once Tosey turned up Banta started to behave perfectly. So that was it - there was nothing in the rules saying a cat couldn't be an escort therefore out to the parade ring went the three of them. Just at that moment Sam turned up to tell Kevin the latest news. She stared wide eyed, amazed to see her husband and the pets acting perfectly as they trotted out in front of the crowd.

The competition involved getting the dog to walk to heel, make it sit, wait for the command then come to
its owner then finally to fetch and retrieve. It was quite a site; Tosey who had very little training did exactly as Banta and both of them did every command perfectly bar the cat actually retrieving and fetching. Sam shouted her support and Kevin was glad that Sam had seen the spectacle. Once back stage (so to speak) the family was back together and Sam and Kevin rejoiced and showed their love of the two animals letting them know they had done well and cuddling them. Kevin asked unaccusingly: "why did you let the cat out of his cage?" and Sam filled Kevin in on the saga with the RSPCA. She said "we better let them know that we've got cat back" but Kevin replied that it was their own fault and to let them stew in it for a while.

23

It was not long until the prize giving for the 'show dog competition', even though the Gwyns knew they had the best response from the crowd, the judges probably would not give Banta a ribbon and it was only out of

curiosity that the Gwyns did not leave early and miss the event. Third place was awarded; this went to a large beautifully groomed glossy longhaired black poodle.

Kevin thought this was their best chance of getting a price gone; so when second place was awarded to a Springer Spaniel they felt disappointed, there was no way the judges would find the Gywns rather disobedient dog with his bizarre companion a serious contender for the top prize of the day. The judge then announced on the microphone "and for first place

we award the threesome of Kevin Gwyn with his Golden retriever Banta and their cat Tosey". Sam jumped with joy and was so proud of her husband and their two pets, as Kevin went up with them to collect their ribbon.

"What a day" she exclaimed as they strode back to the car and soaked up all the attention from the public who seemed nearly as chuffed as they were themselves. Once in the car the Gwyns relaxed and Tosey, Banta and Sam went to sleep as Kevin piloted them back to the Bothy at Castle Bloat. It was as if Banta and Tosey were paying Sam back for making a mess of her drawing room and trailing paint all round the house earlier that year by adding their first place ribbon to the mantle peace.

Story Six

Tosey and Banta on a Camping Holiday

Another year had gone by; the animals were maturing but still had young hearts. Tosey was now four and- a- half years old and Banta was 5, it was every one's favourite time of year - midsummer. It seemed to the animals that life on the estate was getting repetitive, not that they liked brushes with death but they were keen on finding other exciting things to do. Kevin and Sam must have been feeling the same way or they could read the animals minds. One day Kevin came home from work with a bunch of holiday brochures, he absentmindedly chucked them on the kitchen table and said to Sam "it's about time we had a

holiday". Sam was delighted; the idea was spontaneous but was well timed. There were brochures for the Canaries, Florida and even a cruise round the Mediterranean and at the bottom of the pile was a brochure advertising campervan holidays exploring the Highlands of Scotland.

Sam initially thought Florida would be good, they could then visit Disney world but then Kevin thought that would be more fun when they had children. Then Sam thought about the Canaries but they had actually first met in the Canaries and much as it would be romantic, other than sailing there wasn't a great deal to do there, so then it became a toss - up between a cruise or camping trip. The holidays both had their appeal but neither Kevin nor Sam could make up their minds so eventually it was the animals that tipped the

balance and persuaded the couple to choose. It was the fact that you could not take animals on a cruise ship but they would be ideal in a camper van, plus the animals had not been anywhere or done anything in ages and deserved a holiday as much as anyone.

It turned out to be easy to organise, Kevin booked the van a week in advance, and then he got some road maps and marked all the places he thought the family would like to visit. This consisted of going through Glasgow then up the costal root via loch Lomond and Tarbot, where they would spend their first night, then they would go through Glen Coe via Ben Nevis and onward to Loch Ness and Fort William. From Fort William, they would carry on north to the island of Sky where they planned to climb the Culombs. Continuing to the very north of mainland Scotland John O' Groats and then make their way back through Inverness, Saint Andrews, and Edinburgh then finally, home.

So, it was a mild Sunday morning that the family set of for the highlands in the north of Scotland. As usual when the humans were packing their luggage and leaving it in the hall ready for the off, Banta did not know whether he would be going as well. As it happened one of the main reasons the Gwyns were going in the camper van was so they could bring the pets. Kevin had picked up the van the night before and it was now time to load the luggage, animals and hit the road.

The first hour or so was tedious, boring motor ways and as they approached and drove through Glasgow the traffic got bad and progress was even slower than the cruising speed of the already slow van. However once through the city it wasn't long till they got a taste of the mountains as the land became rugged and soon they got to the bottom of Loch Lomond. There was a fair bit of traffic on the small road but they were making good progress; by early afternoon they arrived at the first campsite.

Once settled in at the campsite, the happy campers tied up Banta outside and because the cat was good at getting free from restraints, they kept her in the van. After that, Kevin and Sam walked to a nearby pub, which was quite famous by word of mouth, for a bite to eat and a tankard of ale.

Both Banta and Tosey were disappointed to see their owners head of in such high spirits only to leave them behind. Banta started to bark, he decided that if he was not going to have any fun then neither were his neighbours. On top of that, there were mouth-watering smells from the other campers' barbeques and Tosey and Banta would not get to eat until morning.

There was a young boy who had been let loose in the campsite by his parents, he was to make Banta's night. The boy came up to Banta patted his head and asked him: "what's wrong boy?" Banta suddenly remembered

his friend Tosey who was looking out the van window. He looked sorrowfully at Tosey then simultaneously strained on his lead. The boy named Henry, was naughty and mischievous, aged about ten, with curly black hair and a cheeky grin. Those who knew him better called him Horrid Henry, he unleashed Banta and found the van door open, releasing Tosey too.

This was great for the pets and they worked their way around the campsite getting lots of delicious scraps left over by the other campers. Henry, proud of his companions, took them to where his parents had their tents. His parents were not impressed and asked Henry where he had got them from? The boy lied and said they were strays and he had saved them! the parents shooed of the two animals. What would Tosey and Banta do now?
Theydecidedtofindtheirownerssoofftheytrotteddowntheroadinthedirectiontheyhad

last seen Kevin and Sam head.

It was not far to the pub, the naughty animals would then have to find a way in. They could not read the 'no pets' sign, of course, but when some inebriated clientele opened the pub door the animals seized the opportunity and ran inside at once. Their entry was so abrupt that a busy waitress carrying plates of hot food sent them flying, screamed as the dog and cat tumbled into the bar. The publican was furious, and shouted: "Who owns these animals?" To Sam and Kevin's horror, they saw who these were. "I'm terribly sorry" apologised Kevin, jumping up off his seat, "I don't know how this happened." The publican said they would have to pay for the spilled food and that they were barred from that pub.

Not liking to lose their temper with the pets, the Gwyns did not know the circumstances that brought the animals to the pub. Sam said to Kevin "How on earth did they get loose and how did they find us at the pub? I'm actually quite impressed". Therefore, to compromise the pets missed their bedtime snack, but Tosey and Banta had already had their fill so did not mind at all.

On the following day the travelling family set of north heading for Glen Coe and Ben Nevis, some of the best scenery in Scotland. This took most of the morning; soon they pulled up at a car park of the main road with the intentions of taking in the view and stretching their legs. Kevin and Sam did not know horrid Henry. If they had, they would have noticed the little boy with his parents stuffing his face with a sandwich at the same car park. Henry noticed his friends Banta and Tosey and as they were let out of the car to go to the loo. Henry

went about petting the animals. Sam and Kevin were tired and realised the animals got on well with this boy so they said he could take Tosey for a short work but Banta was to prone to run off so he had to stay in the car while the Gywns had a nap.

It had been half an hour or so when the Gwyns were woken up by an angry looking man with a moustache and a small and worried looking woman with a frown. Kevin opened his window and said "hello" the man said "have you seen my son"? Kevin told them that he had let a young boy go for a walk with his cat half

an hour ago and was surprised he was not back yet. Everyone was worried as there was a mist coming down over the mountain, and their worst fears were that the boy might have got lost while possibly trying to climb Ben Nevis. As it happened, the two couples had reached the right conclusion. Henry with his companion Tosey had decided to climb Ben Nevis and soon found themselves rather cold and surrounded in mist. Tosey had followed the boy faithfully after all Henry had let him free

the night before and he had got a good meal out of it, but Tosey was not happy now he didn't know the way home and was scared and let it show by meowing loudly.

Back at the car park, the two couples were running through the options; call in the emergency services or head up the mountain themselves. Kevin had done a lot of hill walking, orienteering and climbing in the past so came up with a plan. He decided it was worth trying to find Henry and Tosey himself before calling in mountain petrol as the two of them couldn't have got far and if he took Banta between them they had a good chance of finding Tosey and Hendry.

Kevin had seen the direction the boy had set of in before his nap and explained to Banta as best he could what they were doing, as you know Banta is a clever dog and knew he had to find Tosey and he soon picked up the scent. Kevin and Banta did not walk that fast as the mist was getting thicker and Banta had to keep sniffing about, Kevin thought now that the best thing to pin point the lost explorers would be to shout and shout. He did so nonstop, until finally but faintly he heard a young boy calling back, "help!" The young voice shouted and five minutes later Kevin with Banta found the small boy and the cat. Although it was still misty, all four of them were safe back with their families forty minutes or so later.

28

The boy's father was furious, and his mother in floods of tears but ultimately they were happy to have their son back safe. Kevin was relieved especially as he felt guilty that he had let the boy go off with Tosey. Sam said to Kevin "I love you but can we go home now I think we've had enough excitement for one holiday" Kevin agreed, maybe they had. He turned the campervan round heading south for home and ultimately a good rest.

29

Story Seven

Tosey in a Rally

One day an old rally friend of Kevin's called up and invited Kevin and his family to watch him rally. The pets were coming too as there was no one to look after them at home.

Once at the event, they had to be were locked in the car, perhaps irresponsibly of the couple, or because they had to get some fresh air, they had left a gap in the window of the car and it was open just wide enough for Tosey to crawl out of. Tosey strutted round the service area and saw this bright yellow car with flared wheel arches and a spoiler; called a 6R4 it was probably the fastest car there. Tosey hid in the yellow car.

The rally started and Tosey loved the feeling as she sped along and to see more Tosey came out of her hiding place. The driver nearly crashed with surprise but decided to finish the rally even with the cat. The spectators could not believe their eyes as what looked like a cat co - driving in the winning car. At the end of the rally the cat was keen to get back to his family.

The Gwyns had been looking for Tosey, after eventually finding her had not an inkling of where she might have been. Therefore, when Kevin read his rally magazine he was speechless to see a picture of a rally car with Tosey perched on the dashboard the accompanying headline read:

SCOTTISH RALLY CHAMPION WINS RALLY WITH HELP FROM...A CAT.

30

The fact that Kevin used to rally and that his cat seemed to like it equally as much as he got him thinking. He was doing well at work and he had more money coming in than going out, so he said to Sam: "well why not take up rallying again?"

The problem was that Kevin liked to do most things as a family but Sam wasn't to keen on fast cars, there was also Banter to take into consideration. The best idea was to let Sam and Banter spectator. They could also take photographs at the services or pitch in with the mechanics if need be. This would give Banter a good walk going to some of the obscure spectator points and watch their partners race past.

It took Kevin some organising, he had to get a car and a co - driver, he decided that a classic rally car and series was more to his liking the cars were nearly as fast and more fun to drive. His dream car was an e - type Jaguar but they weren't designed to rally. However Kevin was stubborn, he wanted that car in those rallies. Therefore, Kevin found a mechanic who would build the car and add accessories like felt on the dashboard for Tosey to hold on to.

Soon the car was built, now to find a co - driver. When Kevin was young and had taken rallying quite seriously, he had driven with a professional co - driver. Now Kevin was not going pro any longer, he thought that perhaps his older brother Collin who also loved motor sport would like to do it with him. So Kevin asked Collin, who was delighted. He said: " You must be was mad to be rallying a classic e - type

but I also think its genius". Kevin omitted to mention to Collin about the cat, as he was not sure if Collin would go for it, not liking cats for one.

The rally was to be held in Wales and the team set of from Scotland in a big van with Kevin, Sam, Collin, Banter and Tosey with the car on a trailer. On arrival heads turned in all directions, what a car and who brought their pets with them. During the journey Collin, being quite well versed on rallying, said to Kevin that "I've had seen the cat in the last rally via a magazine, though, I'm slightly uncertain I think it might be good fun".

31

Tosey was on a high ever since the car had appeared at the house, it was better than a nip of catnip. Jumping about, she could not really differentiate between all cars but she knew the type of car that makes a lot of noise and goes very fast just like the 6R4. Banta on the other hand spent the whole of the last rally locked
in the car and did not have much fun at all, so he just wined a bit during the journey and secretly hoped he would not have to go in a fast car.

Soon the Rally had begun, Sam and Banta drove to the second service area but the others raced off to do a satisfactory first stage. It was a couple of stages till the next service stop so Sam and Banta went to a good spectator point. Banta found the cars racing past quite annoying and tried to bite the wheels of the speeding cars. Sam made sure he was tied securely to a tree while she snapped away with her cameras for a rally magazine.

Banta suddenly broke out of his lead and as he ran off was hit by a speeding car. He just lay there and Sam ran onto the track while another spectator flagged down the next car. It must have been a higher power that brought the next car to turn up with a driver co - driver and cat. Sam in tears said to Kevin "quickly can
you get Banta to a vet, he's still breathing but is unconscious, looks like there is blood coming from his mouth.

If it had not been for the urgency of the situation it might have been even more comical, but time was against the dog, and everyone was worried that if he did not get the proper attention soon he might not live. They had to stop the bleeding somehow. One thing on the Gwyns side was a very fast car to drive to the nearest town with a vet. The worry was the police but Kevin took the chance and floored it. Ten minutes later the dog was safe, the friendly vet in dark blue overalls had carefully examined him, and other than concussion the vet said: "There was a little light internal bleeding, with careful nursing he should be back on his feet in no time, so don't worry, and he should eat light meals for a while". Kevin and Sam were very

relieved, they had no need to panic. They decided that in any future incidents, they would do some research first.

Weeks later the Jaguar had been left in the garage and Kevin had decided not to have such a dangerous hobby any longer, so had the car set up for fun runs instead, which were still exciting but and safe. As for

the animals, they might have to stay at home in future or Banta anyway, unless he decided that he liked racing after all.

Story Eight

A Boat, a Voyage and a Shark

Kevin had come to a stand still at work, there were just too many boat builders doing the same as him. He had to take a different angle, what could he design that was exclusive, that no one else was doing. Kevin

was sitting at his desk in the cottage; B a n t a was curled up in the corner with Tosey. Kevin loved his pets and was just thinking about how he would like to sail round the world but he could never leave the animals for such a prolonged period of time, all of a sudden, Kevin had an epiphany: ' Why shouldn't I take the animals? By customizing the yacht for pets like Tosey and Banta'. It was also a great business idea, as a niche market he would customise yachts for pets.

Kevin did not have to design a boat from scratch, he was just going to customise his own boat. He began to do some research into how a dog or cat might react on a boat in the sea. This meant taking the pets out on the boat and keeping a close eye on the animals to see what could be added to the boat to make it pet friendly even on long journeys on the high sea.

Kevin had to get Sam's approval, after all the pets belonged to both of them and there was an element of risk considering the Gwyn's yacht would not be set up for pets till after a trial at sea where they pets could be monitored. It could be argued that Tosey and Banta were being used for experiments, but knowing how much they love adventure I don't think Kevin could be classed as cruel. And with this in mind Sam agreed to the venture.

Sam and Kevin did not like to waste time, so the boat trip or voyage was put in to action straightaway. Kevin got out his charts and started plotting a course. A public holiday was coming up soon, as there was going to be a royal wedding and this seemed the perfect time to set sail. Kevin had plotted a course from the west of

Scotland over to Ireland. The voyage should take a day there and a day back, as long as the wind was good they could sail most of the way. The Gywns' boat was very attractive and if Kevin had not been
in the trade could be considered a bit extravagant for a young couple. It was white and red with a tall mast teak decks and was about forty feet long.

Once again, Tosey and Banta were turning heads, as Sam got the pets out of the car and took them down to the pontoon where Kevin was busy preparing the boat and loading previsions. One of the marine officials

approached Sam as she was walking down the pontoon: "We don't allow pets on the pontoon" he said , Sam, knowing that Kevin carried quite a lot of weight in the mariner, explained who her husband was and that
they were taking the animals with them on the boat.

Tosey had excellent natural balance and although not as enthusiastic as Banta looked confident but then Kevin said it would be completely different once under sail. Kevin had designed harnesses for the pets in case the worst happened and one or both animals were washed overboard.

The Gywns set sail with the wind behind them and all seemed well. Tosey and \Banta were initially kept down below in the cabin and Sam watched them while Kevin manned the helm. Surprisingly Tosey seemed to be loving it, jumping about and inquisitive about the vessel, whereas Banta was not having much of a good time and just lay down under the bed, watching her. Banta felt sick, the relentless rocking was not helping. In fact he retched a couple of times. Sam told him "I hope you get your sea legs soon, then you'll enjoy the trip". She could tell Banta was not well and decided that he might feel better up on deck; after all, he had to appear on deck some time. It was a good idea the fresh salt air and cooling breeze made Banta forget his nausea. Next it was Tosey's turn to come on deck, this had the total opposite effect to Banta, Tosey cowed in the cockpit for it was too cold and wet for her outside. Sam put Tosey down below again; after all, it was easier to look after one pet at a time especially on deck.

They were a few hours into the voyage and the boat was handling well under auto helm, Kevin said: "methinks a spot of fishing is a good idea". He got out the fishing rod and secured a lure before casting the line. It was not long before there was a tug on the line and Kevin reeled in a small halibut, there was not enough meat on the fish to make it worth keeping, so rather than just throwing it back in the water Kevin felt ambitious. Using a halibut as a lure there was a good chance of catching something bigger like a tuna.

So once again Kevin dropped the line in the water, it was quite a wait about 45 minutes before anything happened when suddenly there was a tug on the line, and what a tug , Kevin strained over the rod and

with all his strength started to reel it in. Banta was not sure what the excitement was but it was infectious, so he stuck his head out over the side of the boat and began barking loudly at the water. Kevin strained and strained but on only really made progress when Sam grabbed the rod as well.

Suddenly there was a fish or should I say shark at the end of the line, without thinking and being too stubborn not to get a reward for all their work the Gwyns heaved it on board. The shark was about 5 feet long, wade about 35 pounds, and thrashed about with its razor sharp teeth. Kevin who was tired lost his balance and ended up lying on the deck next to the shark and before anyone could do anything, the shark had sunk his teeth into Kevin's chest. Banta went mad at the site of the shark and seeing his owner at risk in turn bit into the eyes on the sharks head. As the shark had realest his grip on Kevin Sam had to act fast she grabbed the spinnaker pole and shoved the shark back in the water, to her surprise Banta went over with the shark. Luckily the dog harness did its job and Sam was able to pull Banta back aboard before he drowned

.More importantly, Kevin was in a bad way; the shark had punctured Kevin's lung and he was struggling to breathe. Sam was in trouble, she could single handed sail the boat but was worried her husband might die if he did not get the right help. As she knew first aid she practiced mouth to mouth on him and managed to resuscitate him. He was soon sitting up, and getting stronger. She then attended her husband's wounds and kept him warm without moving him too much while the boat was hove to.

It had occurred to her make a mayday call and radio the RNLI helicopter, but this idea was discarded, deciding that this would not be necessary nor helpful, after seeing that Gavin was recovering fast and he soon got back to back to his usual self.

She managed to get the got the yacht home with no hitches, while Gavin rested on deck, and kept an eye on the pets while getting a nice tan in the process. It was not long till the Gwyns were back home safe and sound with some unbelievable stories tell to their children one day.

Story Nine

A Cat, a Dog and a Volcano

That winter; Kevin and Sam had found an exciting hobby. It all happened on Collins' estate, an old mine shaft which not many people had explored. Obviously, Kevin and his brothers had ventured a few hundred feet down the shaft but all ran out of bottle once the tunnel got too tight and signs of cave - ins were spotted. It was different though when Sam and Gavin went down the old mine with their pets. That is where they had gone wrong before not having the eyesight that Tosey had and with the sense of direction that Banta had.

The result was a successful mission down the mine but there was a bit of disappointment, as it did not seem go all that deep and there was no hidden treasure. or not that they knew of anyway. Despite this, the Gwyns had caught the bug and Kevin went onto a cave exploring website and looked at books to see how to progress with this adventure. The obvious step was to join a club, so they did. Then there was a tuition period followed by a genuine cave exploring experience. The club had never really considered pets to go down shafts, underground

caves and rivers, but after Kevin explained these were not ordinary pets and he told his fellow cavers what the dog and cat team had done in the past - adventure wise. After this, it was up to Tosey and Banta to prove themselves, and prove themselves they did.

To proceed with an adventure at the same level as the last eight adventures the Gwyns jumped in to the deep end. Every explorer's dream is to descend down Mount Fiji in Japan and be lead into the centre of the earth, and the Gwyns, though relatively inexperienced knew this was their destiny. Some old folk law claimed the devil would rise from Mount Fuji and conquer the planet. This is not what the Gwyns thought but they did expect maybe to find some stalactites, underground rivers and breathtaking natural beauty, vast empty spaces. "Perhaps we might discover some ourselves in the process too" said Sam. "Um said Kevin, once we get good".

There was a lot of organising for the expedition: harnesses, torches, oxygen cylinders, dry suits, first aid kits. Tosey and Banta would be going, it would be easy to abseil the pets down the initial l stages but if there was any under water obstacles the pets would have to wait till their owners came back to pick them up. The Gwyns didn't really have a time schedule but they only took enough food and water for three days and nights underground.

Just climbing to the top of the volcano was challenging, but after leaving base camp early, the team got to the top at about mid -day. First Sam abseiled down deep into the heart of the volcano and once she got the first flat surface she tugged the rope and down came the pets, finally Kevin descended with all the equipment. It was very exciting; "what to do next?" said Sam. There were various options, to carry on abseiling down and risk running out of rope or to follow a tunnel that led off to the right.

The decision was made for them by a diagram and words saying this way. This was a surprise to the Gwyns as they thought they were the first explorers to venture down the inside of Mount Fuji. Any way the obvious thing to do was to follow the arrow pointing them along the passage. Once underground their senses felt different, there was no day or night just pitch black also there was very little noise. These basic senses were going to change again as the team descended down.

It must have been around day two when the first changes to the surroundings were seen. Banta noticed it first and the humans knew something was up because he was barking like a maniac. As they

proceeded, suddenly there was a noise, yes a trickling noise. Kevin said: "no it couldn't be, not this far down under ground".

Sure enough the team turned a corner and there in front of them in a big cavern n was a giant waterfall plunging into a pool. The torches showed up how amazingly pure the water was, not only was it crystal clear but also delicious to taste. This was a good opportunity to guzzle plenty water and refill their flasks.

"The water leaves the cavern down a steep stream m so why not take advantage of this? said Sam". " I have an excellent plan". It was decided that, having brought life jackets with them to inflate them, leaving the pets to find their way back to the surface, they all jumped in the water. It might mean not taking the animals and expecting them to find their own way home but Sam and Gavin knew what good sense of direction the animals had.

Plus there was a team of helpers camped out on the side of the mountain ready to rescue anyone that came within ear shot. With this in mind and not knowing how challenging the rapids would be, the pets were left on the bank and off went Kevin and Sam.

It was lucky they did leave the pets behind because, as the rapids became surprisingly violent and the pets would have surely drowned. Down and down they went and the deeper they got the hotter the water became. The couple had to get out as quickly as possible if they didn't want to get scalded by the increasingly hot water. To get out of the torrent wasn't that easy as there were no banks on the sides.

Suddenly their opportunity arrived as over a water fall they went and into a cool plunge pool, they dragged themselves out of the water onto a sandy beach and collected their thoughts.

Looking around, worriedly: had the person or people who graffitied the wall near the surface come this far, and if so did they die down here as they could not yet see a way to get back, or a light showing a way out

into the open. "However the graffiti does not show any signs of something like that, " said Sam, taking a closer look at it. "Perhaps it would show us the way out?" Kevin said. The strange thing was seeing more tunnels leading from the plunge pool cavern. There were piles of earth by the entrances to all two of the tunnels and there were claw marks in the soil. Could it be a sign of life this far underground.

There didn't seem to be another way out anyway so they would have to take one of the tunnels. Suddenly there was a big splash into the pool and to the Gwyns' horror and surprise out crawled Tosey, followed shortly by Banta. Well that was one thing the Gwyns should have predicted, after all the pets were amazing swimmers and secondly they hated being left out on any potential adventure. Kevin and Sam were delighted happy to see the pets, especially now there might be a possible predator down there with them.

The Gwyns decided it was time to find their way out, they had enough to report to the outside world and they would leave any further explorers with some good advice. Tosey worked out that his owners were lost and with his nose and Banta's sense of direction they were sure to find their way and return safely to the top of the world... The pets could also identify what the animal was that lived down there, it smelled like a mole, so it wasn't dangerous but at the same time it was enormous or a rodent like.

As they continued along the tunnel led by the dog and cat, Sam said "It seems we're going uphill". "yey" said Kevin. We made it". "and so did Tosey and Banta". Sam and Kevin drew some of their own graffiti with sticks and stones in case they planned a return trip, or for other cavers who may find themselves in a similar situation there.

It wasn't for 3 or 4 hours until he explorers got their first look at there underground horses, these were the size of a pony and seemed far more scared of the explorers than the other way around. The group stood there totally still for a few seconds then fled up the passage. Well that was it, they had found far more than they ever expected. Proof that someone or something had gone down the volcano before them; they had discovered an underwater river as well as a new species of animal. Sam took plenty of photos, with the

assistance of Gavin pointing out interesting aspects to photograph.

It was a matter of hours before they found there exit from the volcano; from where they were standing they could see the ledge that they had first abseiled down to. It was only 20 or 30 feet above them, and now as they were nearly at the top their radios could get through to base camp. Send down a rope the message said and soon enough they were all out of the volcano.

It was a matter of weeks later back at the cottage that the Gywns received a bizarre phone - call from an Australian claiming he had ventured down that same volcano 15 years earlier, but like the Gywns never reported the finds as he didn't want it spoilt by tourism. They were not sure whether they believed him, he sounded a bit young to have gone down there 15 years previously.

This is the last recorded memoirs of Sam, Kevin, Banta and Tosey, not to say it was their last adventure. After all they are all still young.

www.ingramcontent.com/pod-product-compliance
Lightning Source LLC
Chambersburg PA
CBHW021001090426
42736CB00010B/1415